PARENTING
IN A SCREEN
SATURATED
CULTURE

DOUG FIELDS
JONATHAN McKEE

TEACHING HEALTHY DECISION-MAKING
TO THE SMARTPHONE, YOUTUBE,
INSTAGRAM, GAMING GENERATION

TABLE OF CONTENTS

ACKNOWLEDGEMENTS

DOUG

This is always the fun part of book writing for me—to pause long enough to say thanks to so many who have breathed into my life to make it even possible to write anything helpful about parenting and kids.

At the top of my list is Fadi & Kim Cheika—two friends I love and adore! They are amazing people who have loved me and served me and challenged me and been so gracious to me and my family. If we had a dedication page—it would be yours.

Every time I write a book I consider how my incredible family deeply blesses and supports me. My wife Cathy is the real parenting expert who quietly shares her wisdom with tenderness and grace to so many. She is definitely a parenting rock-star (as well as the co-author of our book Intentional Parenting)! My amazing children have this unique combination of being fun, slightly irreverent, and Jesus-focused. And they have brought me such joy—and now as young adults, such deep friendship. Torie, Cody & Cassie…
all I've ever wanted to be great at is one thing—that's being your dad (the journey continues).

My co-author on this project, Jonathan McKee, has been a blast to work with! He's funny, passionate, detailed, persistent, smart, a little manic (did I mention persistent?), and cares deeply about helping parents. I'm sure this will be the first of several Doug/Jonathan projects, and I couldn't be happier.

Several of my friends read this manuscript and weighed in with insightful comments and course corrections, and I'm grateful for your partnership: Kim Alexander, Kim Cheika, Joy Frum, Josh Griffin, Charlie Koeller, Ted & Nancie Lowe, Amanda Maguire, Jay Miller, David Peck, Jana Sarti, Shannon Smith, Linda Vujnov. Super grateful to Jason Pearson (pearpod.com) for believing in this enough to design it and make it so readable so families will be helped. I'm super grateful for all of you!

My passion for this project was birthed from the HomeWord Center for Youth & Family at Azusa Pacific University. I'm most grateful for the way Jim Burns has continued to believe in my gifts (and has since I was 14 years old). I also wanted to create something that would be helpful to the leaders we serve through Downloadyouthministry.com. These amazing leaders/youth workers are always looking for ways to help parents, and it's my hope that this gives them another tool to suggest.

JONATHAN

This is fun—taking a moment to recognize some of the family and friends who have made this book possible. Without these people, this book wouldn't exist.

First, I thank Jesus for being the greatest example of love, compassion, patience, kindness, humility, and staying committed to a cause—all qualities I need as a parent!

I thank my wife Lori for enduring with me through our years on this journey of parenthood. It's been a wild ride, and we've learned a lot together. She is definitely my better half.

I thank my three kids—Alec, Alyssa, and Ashley. Alec, especially, because he was our first born… which really means, our parenting Guinea Pig! We learned a lot through trial and error with Alec and tried to brush up our skills for the girls! (Thanks for taking one for the team, Alec.) Girls, we definitely weren't perfect by the time we got to you. Thanks for being patient with us!

I can't thank Doug enough for taking on this project with me. Doug has been really fun to work with. We've passed this manuscript back and forth so many times with edits, tweaks, and additions that I don't think I'd even recognize our first draft. Doug not only brought amazing wisdom and experience to this project… he made it fun. Thanks, Doug!

Thanks to Jim Burns not only for writing such an insightful foreword, but also for being a caring mentor to both Doug and I. You are a true friend.

Thanks to so many of you who looked at this manuscript for us and contributed stories and material. Thanks to my friends Julie, Ron, Sande, Lane, Scott, and Joe. Thanks Mom and Dad for your feedback. And thanks to Adam McLane for his awesome Appendix about Social Networking & the Phone

I've been involved in youth and family ministry for enough years to seldom be shocked. However, on a recent Friday night, speaking to 1,000+ teenagers on the subject of media, I opened my message by asking, "How many of you believe people can become addicted to their smartphones?"

Every hand went up.

I thought, "Wow, they instinctively know about the addictive nature of media."

But their response to my second question is what shocked me. I asked, "How many of you believe YOU are addicted to your smartphone?"

Again, the majority of their hands shot up. Incredible. They knew their behavior was addictive; furthermore, most of them live in families with parents who are really confused and conflicted about these issues.

Every healthy parent today is trying to figure out how to create a media-safe home. I know there were times I wanted to smash my kids' phones or at least hide them. Honestly, I was too cheap to destroy them since I was the one who paid for them. Me and every parent I know are desperate for answers. This is the first generation that desires a common language to handle this relatively new phenomenon.

That's why I'm so happy that Doug Fields and Jonathan McKee have given us healthy answers in this very practical book—and through common language to help us deal with this most important issue. For example, they use the word guardrails to describe how to manage media use. Guardrails is a great word and an excellent descriptor to use as part of a common language that helps us mentor and protect our kids.

In addition, their writing not only speaks to the important media-related issues families are dealing with, but also it's a really good parenting book! Good parenting isn't simply about raising obedient children; it's also about helping kids become responsible adults. This book guides parents to that theme on every page. Doug and Jonathan's parenting philosophy helps us create boundaries with love.

To get the most out of this resource, I suggest you treat it as a workbook. Write your answers to their questions, dialog with your spouse, friends, or small group. Most likely no one sent you to "parenting school"—so you definitely can use this workbook to learn a lot about media, parenting, and even yourself.

One last thought: Doug and Jonathan are the real deal. They have lived what they write about, and they have my deepest respect. Plus, both of these men are incredible communicators, and I found myself laughing at their sense of humor on almost every page. Doug and Jonathan are a rare combination of experts in the field and fellow pilgrim parents trying to figure it out—and they possess more wit and wisdom than most anyone I know. They deal with a very challenging subject in a way that gives you hands-on, practical advice while at the same time making this an enjoyable read. Enjoy and learn from the best.

Jim Burns, PhD.
President of the HomeWord Center for
Youth & Family at Azusa Pacific University
Author of *Teen-ology* and
10 Building Blocks for a Solid Family

INTRODUCTION: PICKING HILLS TO DIE ON

A mom approached me after one of my parent workshops and said, "I'm having trouble with my daughter. She keeps sneaking."

"What's the problem?" I inquired.

"Well, first of all, she got herself a Twitter account on her phone without my knowledge."

"How old is your daughter?"

"She's almost 17. I asked her how she even got the account because I found out that it requires an email address, and I don't let them have email."

"You don't let them have email?" I asked, trying hard not to sound too disapproving.

"Nope, or Internet access."

I decided it was time to interject an opinion: "Do you mind if I share my honest thoughts with you?"

The mom paused for a moment to process my question, then blinked: "Well, no. I don't mind at all. Please do."

"I'm obviously not in your house, and I won't pretend to know the situation," I began, treading cautiously. "But it sounds like you're having problems with rebellion."

She nodded, agreeing wholeheartedly. "Yes, exactly."

"And you have multiple children?" I asked.

"Yes, 15, 16, and 19."

"And you've told all of them they can't have Internet access, email, Twitter, et cetera?"

"Yes, but my 19-year-old now has it all," she added. "He moved out so he could get all that stuff."

"And I think that's the point I want to make," I noted. "And I'm going to be a little frank with my opinion here, so I hope that's okay."

She swallowed and fidgeted on her feet a little bit: "Okay."

"When our kids are 18, they can legally do whatever they want," I offered. "Like your 19-year-old son, they can move out, get cable TV, Internet, email, Twitter, Instagram, YouTube, iTunes… you name it."

"Yeah… I think he's got all of that now," she said, rolling her eyes.

"And he's figuring it all out on his own," I suggested.

She stopped and thought about my words for a second.

I pressed on. "Don't get me wrong. If your kids wanted to start smoking crack in the house or your daughter wanted to have her boyfriend spend the night, then please do say, 'Sorry, not in this house.' That's a battle to fight. If they want to do something immoral, tell them 'no,' and teach them the value behind your 'no.'

"But when you choose to fight the Battle of Email with a 16-year-old, you're going to have a hard time finding Bible verses to support that one. Furthermore, your kids most likely will either sneak and do it anyway or turn 18 and binge on everything they've been missing out on—and figuring it out on their own because they've never been taught how to use Instagram for good, use Twitter for good, or use email for good… and those tools can be used for good."

She began nodding with what I hoped was agreement.

"I've seen it hundreds of times," I continued. "Parents think they're protecting their kids by sheltering them from the real world, and what they're really doing is never giving them a chance to develop real-world decision-making skills. So when they turn 18, they try it all. And no one is there to guide them… no one is there to pick them up when they fall."

I wrapped up my thoughts: "If you're gonna pick a hill to die on… don't look up from your grave and realize you chose the wrong hill."

CHAPTER ONE:

THE MAP

DO I REALLY NEED DIRECTIONS?

CHAPTER ONE: THE MAP
DO I REALLY NEED DIRECTIONS?

Everywhere we go we hear these common struggles from parents about setting rules and guidelines:

> "My kids tell me I'm way more strict than their friends' parents. Is that necessarily a bad thing?"

> "I know my kids need some rules, but I'm just not good at defining and enforcing them."

> "I don't like to hover over my teenagers' every move, so I give them a lot of freedom. But now they're starting to make some really bad choices, and I'm beginning to wonder if I gave them too much freedom."

Parenting isn't easy, and as technology continues to permeate every area of our lives, many parents now struggle to learn how to set rules or limits in regard to electronic devices.

The average age a young person gets a smartphone today is 10.3-years-old. So even if your child doesn't have a phone yet, she probably pleads, "But Mom, all my friends have phones!" Phones only seem to make parenting more difficult. We hear it all the time:

> "I'm having fits with my daughter and her stupid phone. I just want to smash it."

> "I have no idea what my son is doing for hours each day on his social networking sites. Is it okay for a parent to spy on what their kids have been doing online?"

> "My kids don't seem to want to talk to me. The only way they communicate these days is with their thumbs typing into their phones."

> "We thought we were being good parents by getting our kid a phone, and now we never see her eyes anymore… she's always looking down at that thing and 'talking' to everyone but us!"

Do any of these situations sound familiar?

A LITTLE GUIDANCE

The truth is, every parent needs a little guidance navigating the road of parenting. And we are so excited to partner with you and help you in your journey! We speak to thousands of parents every year, and we're thrilled to have another way (this book) to help. Our goals for this workbook include:
- We'll do a little bit of writing… you do a little bit of reading.
- We'll trigger some questions… you do some reflective thinking and writing.
- We'll give you some ideas… you pray and search for the gems of wisdom that will work for your family.

We've provided numerous opportunities to discuss these issues with your spouse, your friends, or even your parent groups (we included small group discussion questions for each chapter in Appendix A at the end of the book). We encourage you to bring other parents into the discussion and glean their wisdom and experience. If you're married, ask your spouse to read with you and engage each other as you move toward some very important decisions impacting your children.

Throughout this workbook you'll get the opportunity to write down your honest thoughts. Don't worry; your words won't be graded or turned in for evaluation! Think of this element as a journal in which you can express candid reflections concerning what you truly feel as a parent. We'll call these little sections "Honest Thoughts," and they'll always be flagged with this graphic:

Throughout this workbook you'll be given the opportunity to write down your honest thoughts. Don't worry, this won't be graded or turned in for evaluation. Think of it more like a journal where you can express candid reflections of what you truly feel as a parent. We'll call these little sections, "Honest Thoughts," and they will always be flagged with this graphic:

 Honest Thoughts:
Let's give it a try! You've just read some common parenting complaints in the indented quotations. What are some struggles you're experiencing right now with setting or enforcing rules and guidelines in your home? They don't have to be media-related (this workbook will move you toward much bigger areas than simply the battle with your kids' screens). We'll provide some broad categories to stimulate your thinking, and we ask you to write down the first thoughts that pop into your head:

-Struggles with social media-

-Struggles with their relationships-

-Struggles with respect or obedience-

-Struggles with their phones/screens in general-

YOUR GUIDES

We (Doug & Jonathan) are big believers in asking for help and then writing down what we've learned. And this workbook is a compilation of much of what we've learned along the parenting road! Both of us have been working with teenagers and helping parents for several decades. Not to mention, we've both raised teenagers of our own—so we've probably experienced most of the same struggles as you.

Both of us will chime in throughout this workbook in different ways. We wanted to give our distinct voices throughout this workbook because we thought it would be more interesting—and because we didn't parent our kids in exactly the same ways. We agree on most areas, differ on a few, and hope our unique perspectives will help more people.

And to make for easier reading, we'll use "bold & black" with our names to let you know who's talking:

Doug: I'm Doug Fields. Whenever you see my name, you'll be hearing specifically from me. I love being a dad! I sure haven't been perfect, but I married an almost-perfect woman in 1985 (Cathy), and we have three amazing kids who—in spite of our rules/discipline/boundaries—have turned out more amazing than we dreamed possible. All three of them have married incredible people, and our Sunday Night Family Gathering is a rich time of laughter and love and some occasional "get off your phone" comments. Cathy and I often look at each other in wonder over how we've been so blessed to have the family we have. And it's become an even bigger blessing with the arrival of our first grandchild. We've loved parenting and are so ready to spoil our kids' kids and invest in their lives in big ways. I'm also extremely honored to share this book with my friend Jonathan—who is a parenting expert and an amazing communicator. (Plus, he's wrong only a few times in this book. You'll see those spots clearly—when he disagrees with me.)

Jonathan: I'm Jonathan McKee. Whenever you see my name, it means Doug finally let me have a turn! I love being a parent, but I'll be the first to admit parenting isn't always easy. Parenting has us laughing one moment and pulling out our hair the next. Raising teenagers does that to you! I was a teenager myself when I met my wife Lori. I fell head over heels in love… and eventually she got there, too. We were married a month before my 21st birthday in 1991, and two years later our first baby arrived. And now all of a sudden we have three grown kids: 20, 22, and 25. And all three are out of the house, and one of them getting married this year. I'm really excited to be co-writing this book with Doug, because his resources and training have been helping me for years! Plus, Doug is usually right… except when he disagrees with me.

Both Authors: Whenever you see word "both", then both of us are talking, which is really cool because our combined knowledge makes us almost as smart as one normal person!

Don't worry. You're not alone. These are all common struggles, and we're here to offer some time-tested, proven help. We don't have all the answers; and if you ever meet someone who claims to have all the answers about parenting… they probably aren't a parent! But, we do have some ideas that have worked for us, as well as for thousands of parents who have already learned
this material.

One of the key attributes of being a good parent is realizing that you don't have all the answers and committing to learn as you move forward. Parenting never ceases to be a learning experience and there are people out there who have navigated the parenting roads who are willing to help.

It's okay to stop and ask for directions every once in a while! Even if you're a man—yes men, even you can get some helpful direction.

WHY IS IT SO DIFFICULT TO SET GUIDELINES TODAY?

Doug: When I was a kid, I didn't have Facebook, Instagram, Satellite TV, or a smartphone in my pocket. I had a CB radio, a black & white TV… and a curfew!

Jonathan: I remember thinking my curfew was waaaaaaaay too early!

Doug: This is nothing new! No teenager ever seems to like the rules or guardrails set up by their parents.

Jonathan: The reason we are writing this is because the number one question parents ask us at our parenting seminars is, "What rules are realistic and actually helpful for my child to become a responsible adult?"

It's a great question. I mean, let's be honest; we've all seen that overprotective "helicopter parent" who hovers over their kid, makes all their decisions for them, swooping down to protect them from real-life consequences.
Everyone knows that approach doesn't work.

Doug: Ha. Well, everyone but the helicopter parent.

Jonathan: And we've all seen that over-permissive parent who allows their kid to do just about anything, which invites moments of triage throughout the teen years.

Doug: Neither extreme is good—overly protective or overly permissive. Caring parents are searching for a healthy balance of rules (or what we refer to as "guardrails") that will protect our kids now, while equipping them to make good choices when they're out on their own.

Both Authors: A healthy, balanced approach sounds good, but what does this actually look like in your own home? We find that most parents aren't really sure what rules/guardrails to set—they don't want to be too strict… or too lenient. And this uncertainty triggers specific questions… like:

"Is it okay to check my kids' text messages?"

"Can I make my son get a job?"

"Is it safe for my daughter to post photos of herself?"

"How long is too long for them to spend on Instagram?"

"Do you change or adjust rules for each kid, depending on their maturity and personality? My daughter is nothing like my son was at this age!"

"Should I make them turn off their phones/screens at night?"

"Can I just smash their phones? It would make my life so much easier!"

GREAT questions! We're going to address most of these in the chapters to come.

Honest Thoughts:
What about you? What questions do you have about setting rules or guardrails for your children? Write your specific questions in the spaces provided:

_____

_____

_____

_____

_____

_____

_____

_____

Are you on this parenting journey alone? Who else is navigating these roads with you? (Your spouse, stepmom or stepdad, your kids' grandparents?) Why do you think it would be helpful to have someone go through this workbook with you?

_____

_____

_____

"Establishing a balanced approach to guardrails is an act of love."

In this workbook we'll discover how parents can establish realistic, helpful, and even lifesaving rules/guardrails for their kids.

GUARDRAILS VS. RULES

From here on out, we're going to switch back and forth with our terminology—sometimes using the word "rules" but most of the time using "guardrails." It's a subtle word-switch but one we've chosen because we believe "guardrails" is more positive… as well as more visual. "Rules" tends to skew negative. "Guardrails" is a more neutral term that's easier to visualize. Guardrails keep us from crashing. They also empower us to drive with confidence toward our chosen destination. Guardrails don't hinder us; they keep us on course. That's the primary goal of "rules"… oops… "guardrails." They're essential for helping your children feel a strong sense of self and become empowered to make decisions while navigating the real world.

Parenting is a learning experience. The more we learn what's best for our children, the more we can guide them… and guardrails help. Guardrails aren't punishments for your children; they protect them from veering off course. Establishing a balanced approach to guardrails is an act of love.

In Chapter 2 we'll look at the road we want our kids to travel. Since guardrails protect us from veering off course, we need to ask an important question: "Where is this road taking us?"

CHAPTER TWO:

THE ROAD

WHERE IS THIS ROAD TAKING US?

In a world where 8- through 18-year-olds devote as many hours plugged in to entertainment media as their parents spend working full time jobs… today's kids are going to encounter distractions difficult to dodge. As a result, parents are left with some big questions, like:

> "What guardrails can parents set to protect their kids from veering off course?"

Jonathan: Many parents with questions want to jump straight into a list of "effective guardrails." I totally understand! As a parent of three, sometimes I just felt like, "Please! Just give me something that works!" or "Give me something that will solve my problem with my daughter and her obsession with her phone!" Good guardrails will help, but there's a much more important question to ask first.

Doug: Absolutely! The latter questions are good, but this one is better:

> "What good are guardrails, if you don't even know where the road is going?"

Teaching Values

Jonathan: This brings up the foundational issue of one's values. As parents, do we just want to enforce rules that our kids will— at best—robotically behave, or do we want to teach values that will last beyond the behaviors and when parents aren't around?

Doug: Think about it: Whenever we present our kids with a rule, the most common response is, "Why?"

That's a fair question from a child, and we believe the best answer should flow from our family values and belief systems.

If I told my daughter she needed to be home at 11 p.m. on Friday, it was natural for her to balk, asking,

> "Why 11? Is there something magical about 11? Does the Bible say, 'Make sure your kids are home at 11?' How come the McCains don't make their kids come home at 11—aren't they good parents? Why not midnight like all my other friends?"

Jonathan: That sounds exactly like one of my kids. I hate it when they're so logical!

Doug: In all honesty, it's a little shortsighted for parents to arbitrarily enforce guidelines. Where's the articulate reasoning behind them? Our values are the foundation upon which good guidelines are built. Our values will confidently supply answers to the "why?" questions.

Let's pause for a few moments to reflect on our own values.

Honest Thoughts:

List some of your values you hope to pass on to your kids:

_____

_____

_____

_____

_____

Where do your values come from?

_____

_____

_____

_____

_____

_____

_____

Describe how these values have affected guidelines in your home. Give an example:

_____

_____

_____

_____

_____

_____

How has that been working for you?

_____

_____

_____

_____

_____

_____

AN IMPORTANT NOTE ABOUT THE SOURCE OF OUR VALUES: We know our readers come from a variety of backgrounds and hold many different values. Our goal is not to tell you what to believe. We are, however, encouraging you to know what you believe and be able to articulate your values before you set rules or guardrails. This will provide you with a foundation so your rules rest on something consistent with your values.

We both believe the Bible offers great values and have chosen to employ biblical values in our homes and in our parenting. We also believe the more you get to know Jesus and depend on Him, the more you'll be able to pass His love on to your children. In this workbook we'll occasionally cite a Scripture reference, noting its practical wisdom and application. Hopefully these examples will help you see how our values are the foundation on which good guidelines are built.

Doug: The best rules and guidelines flow from our values. In the long term, values are more important than the rules. As our kids learn and embrace values, the rules will make better sense.

Jonathan: For example, if our kids have put their trust in Jesus, then hopefully they're putting Him at the center of their lives and seeking to become more like Him. No, they're not going to be perfect, but their decisions will begin to flow from a sense of values and purpose as a follower of Jesus.

Doug: I like that Jonathan, but some parents are thinking, "That's all nice and fine, but my kid can't spell Christianity let alone align his/her life by the teachings of Jesus." What would you tell them?

Jonathan: That's a great question. I would tell that parent, "Hold your britches for just a second, because we're about to get there." In a couple of pages away, we'll provide an example of what it actually looks like to embark on a road paved with biblical values.

Doug: Wow. It's been 35 years since I've heard the phrase, "Hold your britches." Thank you for that journey to the past.

This process makes sense. We aren't helping our kids grow into responsible adults if we simply set guardrails and never talk about the direction of the road. They should know the "why" (values) behind the rules. The boundaries we impose should naturally flow from the "why." These guardrails should help keep our kids from veering off course, but should never become roadblocks to learning healthy discernment.

This process makes sense. We aren't helping our kids grow into Jonathan: Exactly. The "why" is more important than any rule we set. Guardrails are effective when they help our kids go somewhere they understand: "I turn my phone off at night because admittedly it helps me get better sleep. And I love sleep!" The question is, How can we help our kids understand the "why?"

Both of Us: You need to embark on the road paved with your values.

THE ROAD PAVED WITH YOUR VALUES
That might look a little different for each family. For the purpose of this workbook, let's engage a few examples from a family that values a biblical worldview.

If our values are based on biblical truths, then our kids need to be hearing the truth and seeing it lived out by their parents. So instead of just setting up rules like, "No R-rated movies," parents need to consider the deeper and bigger questions:

1. Are my kids hearing the truth from God's Word in our home?

2. Are there times in our day—meals, coffee, before bed, etc.—where I'm building into them and teaching them the ways of Jesus?

3. Are we plugged into a church where we're learning biblical teaching?

4. Do my kids have any other adult mentors who are discipling them and/or encouraging them in their relationships with Jesus?

If the answer to these questions are "no"… the next question would be, "Where is the foundation for your rules?" It doesn't have to align with our biblical worldviews, but where are your values coming from? Are you simply pulling them out of midair? Why is "No R-rated movies" even a rule?"

What good are rules if they don't have any foundation?

Honest Thoughts:
What are the answers to each of the four previous "deeper and bigger" questions in your home? If you answer "yes" for any of the questions, list examples. Write down your honest answers here:

1. _____

2. _____

3. _____

4. _____

What specific efforts are needed to make each of these happen? Or, if they are happening, what might need to change for them to be stronger?

1. _____

2. _____

3. _____

4. _____

This is getting really exciting!

If you're thinking, "What? How is this getting exciting?" you may have picked up this workbook simply looking for easy tips to establish some rules at home to halt the chaos. And so far we haven't set any rules—but we're moving toward something more important and valuable than "Band-Aid" rules that don't stick long term.

Let's be clear: Your previous list of "specific efforts" aren't rules or guidelines. They're practices you can model in your home. If you begin these practices when your kids are young, they'll likely be much more receptive to your guidelines as they grow up watching them in action. However, if your kids are 17, and you've never cracked a Bible in your home and haven't been consistent in your own morality, this is going to be more difficult—and you might have to be a little more strategic. If this describes your situation, please don't give up. That's where authenticity and a strong relationship with your kids will really help. If your kids love and respect you—and they observe your own life changing—then they might be curious about the reason behind the hope that is in you.

Again, the big idea is: Rules and guidelines will naturally flow from our values.

Jonathan: The Bible has been the source of truth in our family to guide our decision-making. For example, when our kids were at school, and they were questioning how to treat others, they might have reflected on the passage that my daughter Alyssa literally painted on her wall:

Do nothing out of selfish ambition or vain conceit. Rather, in humility value others above yourselves, not looking to your own interests but each of you to the interests of the others. (Philippians 2: 3-4, NIV)

Even now as they are in college and careers—as they reflect on this truth from God's Word and rely on His Spirit—they realize they need to consider the needs of others.

Doug: I want us to be really clear that we're not suggesting that if our kids would just read the Bible they won't need any boundaries from us.

Jonathan: Not at all! Parents must be engaged in ongoing values discussions. I want to make sure we help parents see that the Bible provides truth from which much of their decision-making can flow.

Doug: Good! That's helpful clarity. As parents we've got to be talking about the biblical values our guardrails are built upon. Without this ongoing discussion about values, the cultural noise will mute our occasional efforts.

Let's take sex for example.

Jonathan: Perfect! I was wondering when we'd get to sex.

Doug: I'm sure you were. Our kids are growing up in a sexually saturated society. Sex is everywhere! If our kids watch Netflix or TV they will easily obtain a worldview that sex is a common, recreational act. Almost every character on TV and movies regards sex as simply a physical transaction between two consenting individuals (adults and teenagers). This is why parents must have sex talks (plural)… we can't limit our value of sex to one discussion. The world's dialogue is just too loud. If parents aren't talking about it, they're the only ones who don't have a voice.

My wife (Cathy) and I have a value based on God's Word. Take this passage for example:

Flee from sexual immorality (sex outside of marriage). All other sins a person commits are outside the body, but whoever sins sexually, sins against their own body. (1 Corinthians 6:18, NIV, parenthetical phrase added)

We believe that sex outside of marriage isn't God's design. It's not His ideal. So, we (1) have confidence in that value, (2) teach our kids that value, and (3) use spontaneous opportunities (like the pause button during TV shows) to talk about and reteach biblical sexual values.

The message we communicate isn't simply "don't do it because you might get pregnant!" The message always goes back to the "why"… to God's standard. We taught our kids that sex is God's design… it's God's invention. Sex is good. Actually, it's great—but only when guided by God's standards.

Jonathan: You do an awesome job talking about those principles in your book for husbands, 7 Ways to Be Her Hero: The One Your Wife Has Been Waiting For. Seriously. I gave that book to my daughter's fiancé because it teaches those values so well in a real-world context.

Doug: Thanks.

Jonathan: As our kids begin to learn and adopt values, all these rules—or guardrails—will make more sense. Our kids won't just obey a rule because they want to avoid getting into trouble; they will obey a rule because they know it's the right thing to do based on the values they've been taught.

In the book of Romans, Paul talks about this. He writes:

Therefore, it is necessary to submit to the authorities, not only because of possible punishment but also as a matter of conscience. (Romans 13:5, NIV)

Paul makes it clear that followers of Jesus don't just obey rules because they're scared of consequences. They obey rules because they know, in their hearts, it's the right thing to do.

Doug: It's an exciting moment as a parent when we see our kids making their own good decisions based on values they've embraced as their own.

Jonathan: Truly. But as you clarified a moment ago, this doesn't mean parents who teach values don't need to establish boundaries for their children.

Both of Us: Yes, our values are of the upmost importance—but they don't negate the need for some helpful guardrails. Consider two reasons:

1. Our guardrails help provide the accountability that keeps our kids on course. Our kids may have their full intention on not having sex before they're married, but they also may lack the wisdom and discernment to understand exactly what "fleeing" looks like. Your son might not fully realize that hanging out at his girlfriend's house when her parents aren't home is flirting with disaster. Your daughter might not fully realize the pressure a boyfriend can put on her when she puts herself in precarious situations. A simple guardrail like "no boyfriends/girlfriends in the house when parents aren't home" can help keep our kids "on course."

2. Our guardrails help our kids set good habits making wise choices. For example, the Bible doesn't provide a list of everything we can and cannot do (there were some religious leaders in Jesus' time who tried to do that, and Jesus rebuked them and told them they were missing the point).

- What time should our kids go to bed?
- Should junior high boys shower every day?
- Can our teenagers leave their phones powered on and available on their nightstand all night long?

The Bible doesn't address these issues, so parents need to create and enforce some rules that help kids (especially younger kids) learn some basic wisdom.

Parents can help their kids stay on course by setting helpful and realistic guardrails—based on their values and age-acquired wisdom.

Jonathan: Yes, based on their values. After all, guardrails are only as good as the road taken.

Doug: Agreed! Now, before we get to some actual "guardrails," let's first consider a few major landmarks on this road we're taking.

> **Honest Thoughts:**
>
> How would you summarize this chapter in your own words?
>
> _____
>
> _____
>
> _____
>
> _____
>
> _____
>
> _____

CHAPTER THREE:

THE LANDMARKS

WHEN DO I ACCELERATE... AND BRAKE?

CHAPTER THREE: THE LANDMARKS
WHEN DO I ACCELERATE... AND BRAKE?

Doug: In a world where parents are tempted to just smash their kids' phones with a sledgehammer…

Jonathan: Or throw them in a wood chipper….

Doug: Sure Jonathan, nice of you to include our wood chipper-loving parents, too.

Jonathan: I'm an equal-opportunity writer.

Doug: Anyway, it's probably smart to devote some time to considering realistic rules and guidelines that actually help our kids stay the course as they grow into healthy young adults.

Both of Us: Let's take a minute to quickly review what we've learned so far:

In Chapter 1 we simply agreed that we all could use some parenting guidance. It doesn't hurt to stop and ask for directions. There is no perfect parent. We've both made a lot of mistakes… and you will, too.

In Chapter 2 we learned that our guardrails flow from our values. We asked, "What good are guardrails if you don't even know where the road leads?" We must embark on the road paved with our values. In other words, instead of just setting arbitrary rules, parents need to teach their kids the values from which their rules come from. This puts pressure on parents to have and articulate some essential (personal and family) values.

But guardrails are still important to help keep our kids from veering off course. So how do we know what guardrails to set at what age? After all, rules for a 5-year-old look different than rules for 16-year-old.

Which brings us to the issue of "landmarks." Landmarks are simply the moments or milestones along their journey to adulthood where kids gain more freedom as they grow and mature.

Think about every driving journey where you've stopped, got out of the car, and said, "Wow! That's an awesome sunset" or "That's a big canyon" or "That's the world's largest ball of yarn" or (fill in the blank). It's a moment in the journey marked by something special.

A parenting landmark is the same thing (e.g., "At 9 months little Timmy started walking, at 2 years he could go to the bathroom by himself, at 13 years he got a phone… at 29 years he finally got a job and moved out of our basement!")

NO RULES BY AGE 17½

Jonathan: How's this for a landmark? One of our parenting goals for the McKee family was that our daughters wouldn't have any rules by age 17½.

Doug: Okay. You've got my attention. Are you serious? If so, why 17½?

Jonathan: Some parents thought I was nuts. But why wait until our kids are 18 or "out of the house" to get rid of rules? Consider my reasoning:

If we did our job as parents—teaching our daughter strong values, helping her develop discernment, giving her more and more responsibility as she got older—then our 17½-year-old will need very little guidance at this point anyway.

• Our kids are legally free to do whatever they want at age 18, so we may as well set them up to win and let them have a trial run while we're still there to pick them up when they fall.

Doug: Hmmm. Interesting! I knew I wrote this book with you for some reason. I like this idea a lot! But it does trigger some fears and leaves me with questions

> **Honest Thoughts:**
>
> What about you? What is your gut-reaction to Jonathan's "No Rules by Age 17½" idea? Write down your honest thoughts:
>
> _____
>
> _____
>
> _____
>
> _____
>
> _____
>
> _____
>
> _____
>
> _____

Both of Us: Parents need to realize that parenting is a LONG trip and (to continue on this "road" analogy), they need to "plot their trip."

No parent would argue that we use different approaches at various ages along our parenting journey. Think about it: Toddlers need a lot of guidance. If we're playing with our 2-year-old son on the front lawn, and he starts heading toward the busy street, not many parents would just let keep running with an attitude of, "We can't always save him from danger… he's got to learn discernment… let him go. He'll just have to learn the hard way!" No way! Call Child Protective Services! Obviously parents recognize that toddlers need lots of guardrails.

On the opposite extreme, when our kids get to age 18, they can pack their bags, move out, join the Army, and tell us where we can put our rules (hopefully it won't come to this). At this point, trying to impose guardrails feels like too little, too late.

So, are all 18-year-olds ready to make decisions on their own?

Sadly, no.

But the reality is, when your kids turn 18, they can legally move out, get their own place, and begin making all their own choices.

Doug: Let's look at some ways we might "plot some landmarks along the trip" and slowly prepare our kids for real-world decision making by the time they reach age 18.

Jonathan: Or… 17½.

Doug: Right, 17½.

TOO STRICT… OR TOO LENIENT

Both of Us: Some parents don't have their eyes on the calendar. They don't realize that the date is rapidly approaching when their children will be free from the confines of "prison-camp" where they've been raised.

That brings up two extreme parenting styles we briefly mentioned in Chapter 1. Let's take a moment to look a little closer at each extreme.

Extreme 1: The Overprotective Parent: Commonly called the "helicopter parent" because they hover over their kids, swooping down to save them from any of life's difficulties. This overprotective parent enforces so many rules and regulations that their child isn't prepared to make decisions on their own. Instead decisions are made for them. Their world is structured by legalistic rules virtually listed out for them to follow.

…and the list goes on…

We're not hinting that all the items on this list are appropriate entertainment media. We're just saying, "Don't make all the decisions for your kids!" How is this overprotective parenting approach ever going to help children learn discernment? How are they going to make decisions when they encounter decisions that aren't on "the list"?

Healthy discernment comes from a fair amount of pain, experience, and failure. When we save our kids from all types of hurt, we're actually handicapping them and not preparing them to fully live as responsible adults. They will get older—but not necessarily more mature.

But on the complete opposite end of the spectrum, we have…

Extreme 2: The Overly Permissive Parent: Also known as the "friend parent" or the "peerant." This parent has such a strong desire to be liked by their children that they allow them do whatever makes them happy. So their 8-year-old girl is allowed to stream every song she wants; their 12-year-old boy has his phone in his bedroom watching racy Netflix shows Mom & Dad don't even know exist, and their 15-year-old girl has her boyfriend over to spend the night on the weekends. All permissible because that's what the child wants. (Oh, how we wish this were a fictitious example.)

Please! Let's agree that neither extreme is good.

As you can see, parenting styles vary. Some parents enforce heavy guidance while others don't provide any guidance at all. So let's level the playing field and find some common ground that almost every parent would agree with (e.g., toddlers need heavy guidance and 18-year-olds—whether we like it or not—can refuse our guidance attempts completely).

Here's the question every parent must consider: How do we set guidelines that move us from heavy guidance (when they're young) to little or no guidance (when they're 18)?

INCREMENTAL INDEPENDENCE

The answer is a segue. This segue is a gradual decrease from heavy guidance to very little guidance. At various landmarks along their journey, we'll entrust them with more responsibility. This is basically the concept of incremental independence… not total independence. When our daughters turned 5, we didn't give them the keys to the car. And, when our sons turned 16, we didn't let him go on a road trip with his girlfriend for the weekend, even if he promised to be a "good boy."

As parents, we're used to providing age-appropriate discipline and guidelines:

• Toddlers need playpens and cabinet locks so they don't drink bleach.

• Kindergartners usually aren't allowed to walk to the grocery store by themselves to buy treats.

• 5th graders may benefit from time limits on their video games, or they'll never leave the couch and play outside!

• 13-year-olds might need to look up the lyrics of a song and discuss it with their parents before mindlessly adding it to their favorite playlist.

• 16-year-olds may need to turn their phones off at night so they aren't texting until the sun comes up.

These guardrails help our kids stay on course and begin to teach them good decision-making.

For example, consider introducing the guardrail of "co-watching" new TV shows. Good parents don't just label shows "good" or "bad"; instead they teach their kids to think critically about their entertainment choices.

Since our younger kids don't have the maturity to recognize all the subtle lies of the media, we could set up a guardrail where kids watch new TV shows with parents first, discussing the content and its appropriateness. As they mature, they'll be equipped to make these decisions on their own. After all, when they're 18, they can move out and watch whatever they want.

Are you preparing them for that day?

Jonathan: As our kids get older, we will be able to trust them incrementally at various landmarks on their journey with more and more decision-making.

• When my older daughter was 13, we looked at all music lyrics together and talked about songs before she could download them.

• When she was 15, I wouldn't check the lyrics, I just asked her, "Did you Google the lyrics?" She would tell me she had, and we'd talk for a few minutes about the song (it helps that I'm researching this stuff for my job, so I can tell that she wasn't bluffing her answer).

• By 16, I gave her permission to add songs to her playlists without asking, but then we'd discuss it. (It helps that we followed each other on Spotify, downloading each other's playlists. Now she's off at college and we still text each other, "Did you see my new classic rock playlist?")

In short, as my kids grew older, I expanded their freedom at given landmarks.

Honest Thoughts:
What are some examples of when you previously enforced heavy guidance but later offered very light guidance?

_____

_____

_____

_____

Are there some areas in which you might need to lighten up on your guidance? Give some examples of why or why not.

_____

_____

_____

Are there some areas in which, after thinking about it, you might need to increase your guidance? Give some examples.

_____

_____

_____

_____

_____

Are there some areas in which you and your spouse might disagree on how much guidance is needed? (It's a common hurdle with ex-spouses and within blended family situations.) How might you resolve this?

_____

_____

_____

_____

_____

It's good to think about these areas that might need improvement. We're getting closer to the point of actually setting some guardrails (we'll do that in the next chapter).

Doug: The power of this "segue philosophy" from high guidance to low guidance is filled with wonderful opportunities for parent-child conversations. The more parent-child conversations, the better. Binge Netflix together and talk about what you watch (that's the beauty of the "pause" button). Listen to music together and discuss it. Have weekly breakfasts or coffee together and talk about real life. If you save your "talking time" for only when you have "issues" or concerns, then all your communication will come across like "preaching." The more natural, non-judgmental, and engaging the conversations, the better. And the earlier you begin this type of communication with your child, the better.

Jonathan: Then… when your kid hits the landmark of 17½ years of age, you can set them free to make their own decisions… six months early! Think about it:
  • Just six months before they can do it anyway.
  • If you've been talking with them and encouraging them for years, they'll continue to talk with you even when they don't have to! You've already built a healthy relationship with them and will now reap the benefits of safe communication.
  • If they fail at age 17½, they do it in the safety of your oversight, and you are there to lovingly pick them up.

The timing of this concept is significant. As Doug and I were writing the first version of this workbook, my older daughter Alyssa turned 17½. So as the book released and that landmark passed, she finally could download whatever she wanted (but we still had conversations about music), she finally could watch whatever she wanted (and she really didn't watch anything different), she finally got to stay up as late as she wanted (and she was usually tired and went to bed early anyway)… but she was the one making the decisions.

Does this mean I let her have a boyfriend over to spend the night? Nope. We still had "house rules" (and thankfully she wouldn't have done that anyway). We've also made proactive efforts to make our relationship with her a priority. We had family meals regularly, I took her to breakfast once a week, and my wife hung out with her frequently. Alyssa actually seemed to talk with us more as we slowly segued to low guidance. And now that she lives 500 miles away we still talk regularly. Just last week she was telling me about some of the values she was passing on to the small group of girls she mentors.

Doug: Allowing our kids to make the choices we wouldn't make is where it gets difficult. I'm not even referring to moral choices; just choices we wouldn't make. When our youngest was a senior in high school (and during the time I was putting together this workbook), we were talking about a decision she needed to make, and I told her, "It's your choice." And in my opinion, she made the wrong choice. It was about choosing between two events to attend—one with her volleyball team (where she's the captain) and one that was a spontaneous, last-minute ask. When she was younger, we would have made that choice for her because of the finances involved in the team sport, and there wouldn't have been an option. When she asked, "What do you think I should do?" I gave her my opinion and my reasoning, but I clearly stated, "This is 100 percent your choice. And, like all situations similar to this, I promise not to ride you, ridicule you, or demean you if it turns out to be the wrong choice."

That last statement is an important part of parenting. If kids feel like you're going to "hold their choices over them," they'll often appease and meekly make the choice you would prefer. Unfortunately, guilt doesn't teach them healthy decision-making skills. Kids learn to make good decisions by making some bad ones. Then, when they do, they find that there's some "grace space" at home where the pain of the bad decision isn't compounded by belittling comments.

Jonathan: It can be difficult to truly release our grip. But eventually we have to. We're fooling ourselves when we think otherwise.

Doug: So Jonathan and I leave you with this question: Are you getting your child ready for that day when he/she turns 17½? It may seem like a long time away, but don't blink my friend… that day is coming quickly. Your intentional actions now will prepare for better years in the future.

Honest Thoughts:
How would you summarize this chapter in your own words?

_____

_____

_____

_____

_____

CHAPTER FOUR:

THE GUARDRAILS

WHAT RULES ARE ACTUALLY HELPFUL?

Do you allow your teenagers to download anything they want?

Do you monitor their social media use?

Do they have a bedtime?

What happens if they don't do their chores? Talk back? Fight with their siblings?

Are they allowed to watch whatever entertainment they want on their devices?

You picked up this workbook with the hope of learning how to establish rules, and up until now we've focused on the foundation of rules. Now we're finally going to set up some helpful guardrails!

You may be thinking, "It's about time!"

Yep! We understand your eagerness, but now your rules are going to have some teeth because they'll come from the depth of your values.

As we've written, healthy parenting isn't arbitrarily implementing rules that seem to make sense at the time. Setting good guardrails for our children requires some deep thinking.

The journey we've taken together so far looks like this:

1. **THE MAP.** Always be willing to ask for directions. The most effective parents actively look for ways to improve. (Chapter 1)

2. **THE ROAD.** Embark on the road paved with your values. What good are guardrails without knowing where the road is going? Your family values provide the truth from which your decision-making flows. Use numerous avenues to teach your kids values. (Chapter 2)

3. **THE LANDMARKS.** Plot your trip. Setting guardrails is a segue—a gradual decrease—from heavy guidance to less guidance. (Chapter 3)

and finally, in this chapter…

4. **THE GUARDRAILS.** Set helpful and realistic guardrails that help keep your kids from veering off course.

What has this journey looked like for you so far?

Honest Thoughts:
What is one principle or concern that has stuck with you as you've been working through the previous chapters in this workbook?

_____

_____

_____

_____

_____

Have you discovered any ideas you'd like to try in your home? What will that look like?

_____

_____

_____

_____

_____

Okay, it's finally time for us to set up some helpful guardrails. But before you pick up a pen and start writing, here are a few thoughts to consider when establishing your unique guardrails.

THOUGHTS TO CONSIDER BEFORE SETTING GUARDRAILS:
The younger your kids are when you set guardrails, the easier the guardrails are to enforce. Let's be honest—if your kids are now 16 and 17, and they've been doing whatever they want for the last decade… good luck! We're not suggesting it's hopeless if you're in that situation, but let's at least be honest enough to recognize it will be far more difficult to try to curb a 10th grader's technology use than a 4th grader's. If parents set the expectation before their kids get phones, they can get their kids to opt in on the decision-making about phone use (see the sample "Phone Contract" in APPENDIX B at the end of the book).

• The more you involve your kids in the process of setting up guardrails, the easier the guardrails are to implement and enforce. The more you involve your kids in this process, the more ownership they'll feel. They're more likely to support what they help create. We have numerous friends who've written (as a family) a "family constitution" that describes values, guidelines, and clear consequences when guidelines are violated. Again, kids more readily follow guidelines they've helped author (we'll reveal more about how to do this in the next chapter).

• Ask yourself: Do these guardrails help teach our kids discernment, or do they "do all the thinking for them"? Whenever possible, consider making guardrails that help your kids think through the decision-making process.

• For example: If you make a rule requiring your kids to talk about the lyrics of a song before adding it to their favorite playlist, that might open the door to teach them about discernment and equip them to make those types of decisions on their own some day.

• Now, please note that this isn't fool proof. When parents say, "Bedtime is 10 o'clock!" that won't necessarily teach them to think through healthy sleep habits. That's when parents step in and help them think through the decision-making process. Kids learn to make good decisions by making good decisions. We, as parents, must give them opportunities to practice making decisions. Remember: children learn to make good decisions by making some bad ones along the way.

• Ask: Do these rules provide opportunities for us to dialogue with them? Most kids prefer a chance to talk about something rather than just stand at attention when you bark out rules. A guardrail that prompts them to talk with you becomes a great opportunity to spend more time in conversation.

• Ask: Is this guardrail really motivated by a desire for my kids' development or is it more for my convenience? Sometimes parents create specific rules out of selfishness, rationalizing it as "best for the kids." For example, some Christian parents might make a hard-and-fast "no secular music" rule because, in all honesty, it takes a lot of work to talk about lyrics and teach discernment. (Be careful. If you settle for this rule, then your kids can't sing evil, secular songs like "Happy Birthday" or "Row, Row, Row Your Boat.")

• The answer to family trouble isn't establishing more rules. When tension and trouble arrive, many parents' natural, typical response is more "rules." Their reasoning becomes, "More rules equal better behavior." Nope! The best rules are created in the context of relationships. If you work hard at communication and developing a relationship with your child, both rules and consequences are easier to enforce.

• When setting entertainment media guardrails, include "co-viewing" as much as possible. Which would you prefer? (1) A general rule like "No PG-13 movies!" or (2) "Let's look up this one and see what it's about. Then let's watch it together and discuss it afterward." The latter idea will require more time (and won't always work), but it will create an environment in which your kids realize you're not simply pulling rules out of thin air.

In addition, a co-viewing approach to parenting models discernment and decision-making and will prepare your children for times when their friends (who may be able to watch anything they desire) want to watch something unacceptable in the face of your values.

For example, inevitably you'll receive a phone call from your kid—when she's spending the night with all her friends—because her friend's uninformed parent is allowing the sleepover group to watch an inappropriate film (that appears "okay" to the parents because they've bought into the world's perspective that PG-13 movies can't be that bad). That's when you have to make a really tough decision. Do you make your kid face the potential humiliation of being the only girl who isn't allowed to watch that garbage, forcing the whole group to watch God's Not Dead XI?

That type of scenario makes parenting difficult. But it also will prepare you to proactively communicate with other parents about their plans. Also, it will clearly communicate to your own children that you deeply care for them (although they won't appreciate it at the time). Rules communicate love. A rule-less environment leaves children feeling unloved, despite how much they don't appear to like them.

• Set age- and gender-appropriate guidelines. If we're talking about media guardrails, realize boys are more visual, and girls are more emotional. If my boy was 15, he would be waaaaaaaaaaaay more affected by all the sensuality of some films, and I would probably set different guardrails than I would with my 16- or 17-year-old daughters. So if she calls me from her friend's house wanting to see a PG-13 film that I know is a little sensual, I might reluctantly choose to let her make the decision, and not have her suffer that embarrassment. I might tell her, "I've heard that film is trash, but I'm going to let you make the call on this one. Let's just connect for lunch tomorrow, and you can tell me all about it."

Those aren't easy situations. That's where good values and a segue (a gradual decrease from heavy guidance to much lighter guidance) will help as you make those on-the-spot decisions.

SIDE BAR

Lane, divorced father, writes about co-parenting in divorced or blended homes:

The end of marriage is enough of a challenge for any person to work through, but when you add a co-parenting responsibility with an ex-spouse who has a different philosophy of raising children; it can feel like an impossible road.

But it isn't.

If you're in a similar situation, here are a few tips:

1. Let go of the need to manage your ex-spouse's home. Even if your style is more effective, the harder you try to change your ex, the more entrenched he/she will probably become in his/her methodology. You only have power in your own home.

2. Don't criticize your ex. This only opens the door to competition between spouses and gives kids leverage to pit you against each other.

3. Create a culture of boundaries and accountability. Don't be manipulated when your kids say, "But Mom/Dad lets us do this!" Set your boundaries for your home.

4. Pick your battles. If your kids are allowed to do something in your ex's home, think carefully before banning it in your home. You'd better have pretty good reasons to fight that war (because that's what it may become). Don't underestimate the power of just being a positive influence, teaching values, and hoping your kids eventually make the right choice on their own.

Honest Thoughts:
Which of these pre-guardrail-making considerations challenged your thinking the most? Why?

_____

_____

_____

_____

_____

Will any of these change how you set guardrails in your home? Which ones? Give specific examples.

_____

_____

_____

_____

_____

So enough with all the "pre-guardrail" conversation. What are some good guardrails?

Please note that we don't believe our guardrails are the correct guardrails for all families. We list them only to serve as examples that might help you create your own.

We actually hesitated to list examples because it almost defeats the purpose of what we've been trying to teach—learning how to set up guardrails from your own values and teach discernment. So please don't simply adopt ours without any thought and prayer. Use the process we've been talking about in these chapters and come up with guardrails that fit your particular situation.

Both of us have talked with other friends about guardrails that have worked in their homes. We've learned from others and adopted and adapted some ideas from them. It's shrewd to glean wisdom from others (especially those who share your values). You might glean a few of ours—and that's okay, as long as they fit your values and situation.

Here are just a few of the guardrails we've used with success.

SAMPLE GUARDRAILS:

Doug: Here are four examples of guardrails we applied in the Fields family:

• We connected specific guardrails to being responsible with time. For example, we had curfew times. We also articulated certain times and days for doing chores. S, rather than saying, "Take out the trash sometime this week," the chore was "trash is emptied every Monday, Wednesday, and Friday). If those times/days were missed, there were consequences (which our kids knew ahead of time). We even put time limits on TV and video games and playing with friends on school days. We found that if we emphasized specific times and made those expectations clear, we didn't have to nag. If one of our kids chose to miss their time window—key word: chose—the consequence would kick in. Easy!

When the guardrails are known ahead of time, and the consequences are clear, it becomes a lot easier for parents to enforce the consequences. We didn't have to yell and scream and threaten and nag… we simply had to impose the consequence (which isn't easy, but it got easier the more we followed through and the more our kids realized we were serious about consequences).

• Mom and I could check Instagram, text messages, etc., any time we want. Today's kids think they have a right to privacy. Yes, they have a right to change clothes in their bedrooms without us barging in, but no, they don't have a right to chat with some 16-year-old model they met from Orange County via Facebook (who's really a 44-year-old, naked, hairy, serial killer living in his parent's basement in Cleveland). Kids who were raised on Disney shows—in which all parents are characterized as morons and kids rule the earth—might not believe this rule is fair, but it's for their own good—especially in the early, formative years of learning discernment. We have their passwords and access to their social media. By the way, this was an easy rule for our kids to agree to when each of them claimed to be "the only one" in school without a phone. While we knew that was an exaggeration as well as an attempt at manipulation, our kids were eager and desperate enough to agree with our predetermined phone rules.

• Phones are turned off at night. Research reveals that kids need 9 hours 15 minutes of sleep per night, and they average 7½. Technology takes a lot of the blame for this. One recent study showed that among 13-to 18-year olds, one in 10 is awakened at night by a phone call, text, or email. And 28% of this age group leaves their phone ringers on all night. (Check out the National Sleep Foundation's Sleep in America® poll). So, do your kids a favor and make a rule that the phones are turned off at night. If it's too much of a temptation (and it probably is), simply keep a charging station in your bedroom where your kids "check-in" their phones every night.

• No computers or tablets in bedrooms. Our home computer was out in the open in a common space. This—along with the guardrail of no phones at night—really helped kids avoid the temptation of browsing somewhere dangerous. This guardrail is actually backed by countless American Academy of Pediatrics reports that strongly recommend no screens in kids' bedrooms.

Jonathan: That's a great list, Doug. We actually had three of those in our house as well. Here are four more examples of guardrails that we applied in the McKee family:

• Do your chores without being asked. Don't wait for us to tell you to make your bed. If we have to ask you, then your list of chores will increase.

• We discuss music before downloading or adding it to your playlists. Yes, we allowed secular music in our home. If you look at the Billboard charts right now you'll probably find some clean stuff. I didn't say "no" to this stuff. My kids and I had some good conversations about these songs. We also had some conversations about some of the inappropriate songs. We didn't have to say "no" to many of those because our son and daughters decided "no" for themselves. And, interestingly enough, my kids actually said "yes" to some pretty good music, including some worship music. Both of my daughters still regularly listen to worship music. In fact, I follow one of Ashley's cool Christian music lists on Spotify.

• Only one hour of video games on school nights. Like many parents, we found this "screen time limit" helpful and necessary or homework never would have been accomplished.

• No "friending" others on social media they haven't met face-to-face. Sorry, I don't care if he seems like "the nicest guy ever." If he's nice, he can meet me face to face and prove he is who he says he is.

Then there are guardrails Doug and I enforced differently. I wouldn't say we disagree on these—we just had different approaches. For example, in the McKee house, we always had a guardrail that our kids' doors must remain open when those of the opposite sex were in their rooms.

> Doug: In the Fields' house, we had a guardrail that no kids of opposite sex were allowed in bedrooms at all!

> Both of Us: But we both agreed that no friends of the opposite sex are to be inside the house when parents aren't home.

> You'll often find different families with similar morals and values have different guardrails. This is okay.

> Hopefully these examples will stimulate your thinking about some guardrails that will work in your own home.

Honest Thoughts:
Which of the aforementioned guardrails do you like?

_____

_____

_____

_____

Which of them might be difficult to introduce in your home? Why?

_____

_____

_____

_____

What are other guardrails you might want to include in your home?

_____

_____

_____

_____

_____

ACTUALLY WRITING DOWN GUARDRAILS
This whole workbook is about guardrails. We've discussed values, landmarks, pre-guardrail considerations, and now some actual guardrails. We've even written out a few you might consider adopting in your home.

Now let's spend a few moments thinking about how to sit down and write out an official list of guardrails.

GUARDRAIL WRITING TIPS
Here are some ideas to help you think through what guardrails you want… and don't want. We've provided some space for you to brainstorm and write your thoughts after each one:

• If your relationship with Jesus is important to you, then begin this process in prayer. Ask Him to guide you through this important time. Ask specifically to help you come up with realistic guardrails that flow from His word. Also ask Christ to give you the wisdom to notice and steer clear of legalism.

• List some values in your home that might need some realistic guardrails to protect your family. For example, if you value sexual purity, maybe you see the need for some guardrails to make sure technology isn't inviting temptations into the house. Write out some realistic guardrails that flow from these values.

_____

_____

_____

_____

_____

• List some rules you have observed as legalistic or unfair that you want to avoid. Ask: Why are they unfair? Why don't these rules work? It's not bad to be reminded of what doesn't work.

_____

_____

_____

_____

_____

• List some guardrails you grew up with that you might want to adopt.

_____

_____

_____

_____

_____

• List some guardrails you grew up with that you might want to burn in a bonfire!

_____

_____

_____

_____

• List some guardrails you've read about in this workbook that you may want to adopt.

_____

_____

_____

_____

• List some guardrails you've observed in other families that are attractive to you.

_____

_____

_____

_____

• List some guardrails you've seen elsewhere that you never want to adopt!

_____

_____

_____

_____

• Allow your family in on the conversation. Let everyone know you're considering setting some helpful and realistic guardrails for the family. After all the moaning and whining is done, tell them you're interested in everyone's input. Ask questions at the dinner table like, "What are some realistic guidelines we should have for phone/screen use in our house?" See what they come up with. Propose some of the principles you've learned in this workbook and ask for their responses. The more you involve your kids in writing down the guardrails, the easier it will be to implement them.

• Ask parent friends about rules or guardrails in their homes. Which ones have been successful? Which ones are they struggling with?

_____

_____

_____

_____

• If there are two parents in the picture, and your spouse hasn't been involved in reading this workbook, gently bring up this conversation and ask if he/she would like to go through this workbook with you. Ask your spouse to brainstorm some guardrails with you.

_____

_____

_____

_____

Once you've written down some of these potential guardrails, run them through this pre-trip checklist:

❏ Do these guardrails start with heavy guidance and segue toward lighter guidance?

❏ Do these guardrails help teach discernment, or do the rules do all the thinking?

❏ Do these guardrails create opportunities for dialogue?

❏ Are these guardrails really motivated by a desire for my kids' development, or are they for my convenience?

❏ Do these guardrails encourage co-viewing of entertainment media?

❏ Are these guardrails gender- and age-appropriate?

Keep your list to fewer than 10 guardrails. You don't need to make a rule for every situation. That's where values kick in. If you're teaching your kids about purity, you shouldn't have to have several purity rules (e.g., "No going to second base with your girlfriend").

If you have more than 10 guardrails, you're going to frustrate your kids and your guardrails may be harmful and border on legalism. Trim! Besides, certain gadgets are going to require their own sets of guardrails. When your kid learns to drive, a whole host of new rules, many enforced by law, will enter the picture. Therefore you needn't include "no speeding" in your list of guardrails.

In the same way, we encourage parents to introduce a phone contract when their children first get phones (we've even included a sample in Appendix A). So don't worry about trying to foresee every phone danger when composing your list of guardrails.

Finally, we encourage you to finish the last two chapters of this book before confirming your list of guardrails. These chapters will offer numerous opportunities to think about the real-world implementation and application of your guardrails and help you edit, trim, or add to them.

These tips should help you in the process of writing, editing, and rewriting an almost-final list of proposed guardrails for your family.

 Honest Thoughts:

Which of these aforementioned tips might be the most difficult to carry out? Why?

_____

_____

_____

_____

_____

Sometimes it helps to make a plan. Write down a time in the next few days where you can start to implement some of these tips and begin writing down your "almost-final" list of proposed guardrails for your home.

_____

_____

_____

_____

_____

We've come a long way.

We've looked at the map and realized we need directions. Then, using common sense, we agreed that it would be ridiculous to focus on guardrails without first considering where the road was going. So we spent some time thinking about our values and how our rules and standards will flow from those values. Then we plotted our course, planning a journey from heavy guidance to lighter guidance. Eventually it was time to set realistic and helpful guardrails, so we spend some time compiling that list, editing it, tweaking it—and now we have an "almost final" list of proposed guardrails.

This is all good, but it's also all a bunch of theory… until we actually drive on the road. This means implementing our guardrails.

IT'S TIME TO SHIFT INTO DRIVE.

Doug: So, apparently this is an automatic transmission?

Jonathan: I guess so. Otherwise we would have said, "Release the clutch." I don't know if that has such a good ring to it.

Doug: It might fit for legalistic parents!

Jonathan: Clever… touché.

Doug: Let's consider what it looks like when we present our "almost-final" list of proposed guardrails to our families. We need to be aware that some family members might have some difficulty accepting these new guardrails.

Jonathan: I agree. As we mentioned earlier, if you have a 16- and a 17-year-old who've had free reign for the last few years… rules might not come easy.

Doug: Hopefully this process will have helped those particular families write "lighter guidance" age-specific rules. But still… it admittedly will be easier when families begin this process with younger kids.

Both of Us: So, what does introducing these guardrails look like? In other words, how do we get from our "rough draft" guardrails (that we've been creating) to actual, functioning "final draft" guardrails that we'll implement in our home?

YOUR 10 PROPOSED GUARDRAILS

We're going to provide you space on the following pages to write down your "almost final" list of proposed guardrails. We've provided a place to create 10 guardrails. Don't feel the need to fill all 10 spots. At the same time, as mentioned previously, you probably don't want to exceed 10 guardrails.

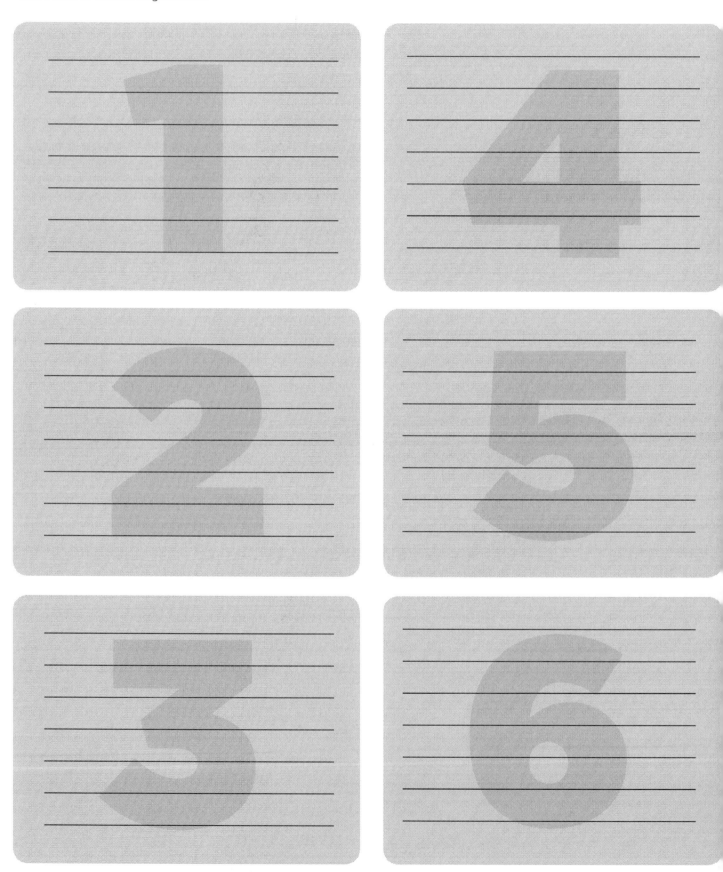

Don't rush this process. It might take a few weeks to take all these steps as you pray through the process, write numerous drafts, and involve your family. But eventually you'll come up with an "almost final" list of proposed guardrails.

In the next chapter we'll show you how to present this list to your family.

Don't worry… you'll be great! We understand how tough it is "change things up" within your family dynamics. But it's worth the fight!

📢 **Honest Thoughts:**

How would you summarize this chapter in your own words?

_____

_____

_____

_____

_____

ENDNOTE: You can actually get a glimpse of what that conversation looks like in Jonathan's parenting book, *Candid Confessions of an Imperfect Parent*, in Chapter 6, titled, "Dad, Can I Download This Song?"

CHAPTER FIVE:

DRIVE

HOW DO I IMPLEMENT THESE GUARDRAILS?

INTRODUCING GUARDRAILS TO YOUR FAMILY

We encourage parents to begin the initial conversations using language that communicates these as "possible guardrails." We're not suggesting you back down if your kids don't like the rules, or they react poorly. We just believe it's better to slowly walk into the "rules pool" rather than an out-of-nowhere cannonball. You might consider using the word experiment, especially if your kids are older, or if you're concerned your family will freak out. An experiment doesn't communicate finality, and you can easily abandon experiments that don't work. And even if you don't plan to ditch it, such terminology can be an easier way to communicate upcoming changes that will impact lives.

Be ready to listen. Don't be defensive. Don't get baited into arguing and/or yelling (which never works). Simply communicate your excitement for some needed direction and clarity for your family. Don't feel the need to answer every objection. It's okay to respond, "That's something worth thinking about. I really appreciate your feedback. We'll talk about this again next Monday night. I want the weekend to reflect on your thoughts and pray about it."

Doug: Hopefully this isn't the first time your family has heard about your movement toward some guardrails.

Jonathan: If you've taken our advice from the last chapter in our section with tips for writing down guardrails, you've already been talking with your family about "hypothetical" guardrails and getting feedback along the way. That feedback has probably already resulted in a few tweaks here and there.

Doug: So basically what we're suggesting is that these guardrails shouldn't be a total shock to your children.

Both of Us: Here are four steps we've found helpful for introducing your list of guardrails to your family.

Introducing Your List of "Proposed" Guardrails to Your Family

1. SET A TIME FOR A FAMILY MEETING.
Introducing Your List of "Proposed" Guardrails to Your Family

• Set a time for a family meeting.
Don't just spring guardrails on your kids on the way to school some morning:

"By the way Chris, when you get home, don't plan on staring at your phone all day. We've canceled Netflix and are now limiting screen time to just 1 hour a day! Have a great day at school!"

Good luck with that approach!

Set a time when you can sit down with your family and introduce the list of guardrails you've compiled.

Consider making it a fun location. Maybe you take everyone to a favorite ice cream parlor. Joke with them about how you're going to get them dosed up on sugar before you drop the "guardrail bomb" on them. A neutral, public setting usually doesn't allow for anger to escalate.

2. HAND EVERYONE A PRINTED COPY.
Print the list of your guardrails and keep it to one page so they aren't overwhelmed. If your guardrails take more than one page, you might want to consider trimming the number of guardrails you've compiled (revisit the tips from the last chapter about keeping guardrails under 10).

3. INTRODUCE THEM AS "PROPOSED" GUARDRAILS.
As you hand out your list, say, "Here's the list of proposed guardrails your mother/father and I have created." Just like the word experiment is defusing, the term proposed suggests potential flexibility. It conveys that the conversation is open and ongoing.

You'll want to keep the channels of communication open in your home and encourage dialogue. Conversation is the fuel for strong parent-child relationships and where wisdom is passed on.

4. ASK FOR FEEDBACK.
As you hand out the list of "proposed" guardrails, ask for feedback:

"Take a look at this list of proposed guardrails. As you know, we've been asking you about some of these for the past two weeks, so all of these shouldn't be surprising. Let's go through each one, and we want to know what you think."

The goal is to not surprise everyone in the family. As we've noted before, the more you involve your family in the process of writing the guardrails, the easier it will be to implement them. We've seen numerous families go through this process together—in which the kids really did help write the guardrails—and the guardrails became more of a "family constitution" for which everyone was able to take some credit.

As the family looks at this list and offers feedback, don't feel the need to make an immediate decision. Listen to the feedback, discuss it as needed, but then feel free to finish with, "This is something your dad/mom and I will continue to discuss and pray about. We'll make a final decision in the next 48 hours." Be clear about when it's "go time" and don't be afraid to make the final decision. You're the parent, and your kids need you to be a strong, loving, thoughtful parent.

As you can see, this journey began with just you—or you and your spouse—and then slowly extended to become an interactive process with the entire family. The interaction you'll experience dialoging about some of these guardrails is an important part of the process. Make every effort to make it a pleasant one. Pray for your attitude. Prepare your responses if your kids display bad attitudes.

As the family looks at this list and offers feedback, don't feel the need to make an immediate decision. Listen to the feedback, discuss it as needed, but then feel free to finish with, "This is something your dad and I will continue to discuss and pray about. We'll make a final decision in the next 48 hours." Be clear about when it's "go time" and don't be afraid to make the final decision. You are still the parent and your kids need you to be a strong, loving, thoughtful parent.

As you can see, this journey began with just you, or you and a spouse, and then slowly extended to become an interactive process with the entire family. The interaction you'll experience dialoguing about some of these guardrails is an important part of the process. Make every effort to make it a pleasant one. Pray for your own attitudes. Prepare how you'll respond if your kids display bad attitudes.

> 📢 Honest Thoughts:
> How do you think your family will respond to your list of "almost final" proposed guidelines?
>
> _____
> _____
> _____
> _____
>
> How might it help to involve your family in this process?
>
> _____
> _____
> _____
> _____
>
> What's scaring you right now about this idea? Who's an experienced parent you might be able to talk to about your fears? What will you ask that parent?
>
> _____
> _____
> _____
> _____
> _____

Jonathan: We've had "family meetings" in our house since the kids were really young. It's always been a fun dynamic. Everyone gets a turn to talk, from youngest to oldest. The kids always felt like they had a voice. Anyone could call a family meeting, but when we met, everyone got a chance to speak. The meetings were always dialogues, not monologues.

It was during one of these family meetings when I first introduced our guidelines, including the one about video game limits. That item stirred up a little discussion, but the family all agreed that it made sense.

It was at one of these family meetings where I first introduced our guidelines, including the one about listening to worship music the first and last hour of every day. That item stirred up a little discussion, but the family all agreed that it was worthy trying.

Doug: That's the good thing about this "proposed" list. It's something to try. If you sell it as just that, then these rules won't feel like a lifetime sentence to solitary. But, no matter how graciously you communicate this, your kids aren't going to jump up and down and thank you for loving them so much to give them guardrails—especially teens. There were times when I went into this family meeting and came out feeling like I was the worst parent in the world.

Both Authors: Don't let this stifle you. Kids need their parents to establish guardrails and hold them accountable. Just remember: while all kids need rules (and really want rules to feel safe and secure and loved), no kids will affirm you for implementing them.

QUESTIONS PARENTS DON'T KNOW HOW TO ANSWER

Sometimes after we've implemented our guardrails, our kids will ask us if they can do something our guardrails don't cover. These are the times you'll be thankful for values guiding your decision-making. Life is full of moments where we need to apply wisdom and values on the fly.

Sometimes our kids will stump us. For example, your kids might ask if they can have a specific app… and you have absolutely no idea if it's a wise decision.

So what do you do then?

Doug: Jonathan, I think it's worth noting that parents don't have to feel the need to become entertainment media experts to put good guardrails in place. In fact, I'll quote you, "We just need to be willing to walk through this with them." I love how you lay out what that actually looks like in the final chapter of your book, If I Had a Parenting Do Over, specifically when you advise parents, "You don't have to become an expert on every app; you just need to be able to say, 'Let's check it out together.'"

Jonathan: Thanks Doug. I think it's comforting for parents to know they don't have to have all the answers. And if their kid asks, "Can I have Snapchat?" parents can simply answer, "I don't know; let's check it out together." This process of looking at entertainment choices together will teach them how to apply values to real life on the spot. Because while our guardrails won't cover every app, movie, and situation, our wisdom and values will. And isn't that what we hope our kids use when they're out on their own?

You're almost done! Only one chapter left. Now let's look at how guidelines like this work in your home.

Doug: Okay, let's review: Once you introduce guardrails, your children will squeal in delight, plaster on huge smiles, and everything will be perfect in your house from that day forward.

Jonathan: Ha! Oh man… that's funny.

Doug: Yeah, it was hard to even write that with a straight face.

Jonathan: The reality of the situation is that rules will always be broken and boundaries will always be pushed.

Doug: Yep, they sure were in my house. As parents our job is to be prepared for how to handle those situations when they happen.

Jonathan: Let's look at a common problem: Specifically parents who just want to smash their kid's phone. Here's an actual question I received from a parent:

"Given my daughter's pattern of irresponsibility with her phone, I'd love to just cut it out of her life altogether. But the drawback is she won't learn how to handle it on her own someday. What do I do?"—Dave

Both of Us: This question provides a perfect opportunity to put some real-world application into this workbook. Well-placed guardrails are a proven tool to proactively keep our kids focused on the road ahead, but they aren't foolproof. Kids will still push boundaries, bust through guardrails, and steer off course.

Let's consider one specific issue that's growing out of control. What's a solution for Dave and other parents whose kids are pushing their luck with their phones and other screens?

A wood chipper?

A sledgehammer?

Sure, those are both potential short-term solutions … but are they good ones?

CHAPTER SIX:
REAL WORLD APPLICATION
WHAT IF THE RULES ARE BROKEN?

If you've been in Dave's position, you can understand his angry response.

Doug: Actually it would be a lot of fun to use a sledgehammer, but I'm also curious about the sound a smartphone would make when going through a wood chipper.

Jonathan: Let us suggest a solution that doesn't kill their phones or maim our relationships with our kids.

Both of Us: Instead of just considering how to respond to misuse of phones and other devices with screens, let's first consider prevention. In other words: What are some good ways to avoid this situation in the first place?

PROACTIVE PARENTING—BEFORE THE INFRACTION
Let's try three steps based on some of the principles we've learned. A little of this will be review, but that's okay since it uses a real-life example of what this entire process might look like:

1. Embark on the Road Paved with Your Values
We suggested that our guardrails are only as good as the road we're on. Phone use guardrails are no different. If we are NOT teaching our kids values, then how can we possibly expect them to make good decisions with technology?

Young people are discovering numerous creative ways to get into trouble via their phones, especially now that the majority of 10- to 17-year-olds have phones with Internet access, apps, an entire music library, videos… you name it! Here are some of the common ways kids wander into trouble with their phones and other screen devices:

- texting/chatting too much
- engaging in inappropriate conversations they probably wouldn't have if they were face-to-face
- sacrificing time with friends/family for time on the phone
- spending too much time on social network sites
- spending too much time gaming
- streaming raunchy music or YouTube videos
- browsing racy apps, stories, or websites
- exchanging inappropriate images
- getting into exchanges where it's easy to bully or be bullied

If we're teaching our children values, many of the latter scenarios can be prevented. For example: If they've embraced the biblical concept of purity, then they'll hopefully recognize impure content and have a better chance to flee.

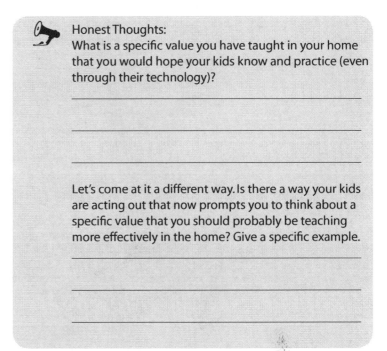

Honest Thoughts:
What is a specific value you have taught in your home that you would hope your kids know and practice (even through their technology)?

_____

_____

_____

Let's come at it a different way. Is there a way your kids are acting out that now prompts you to think about a specific value that you should probably be teaching more effectively in the home? Give a specific example.

_____

_____

_____

_____

It would be nice to assume that our kids are absorbing all our good values and steering away from all temptations. But let's be real. Sin is alluring, especially sexual sin. So…

2. Set Realistic Guardrails
Even when we're modeling and teaching good values, well-placed guardrails often will keep our kids from wandering into dangerous territory.

The phones most kids have in their pockets can access all these online hazards. So what are guardrails that might help kids steer clear of some of these mobile dangers? Consider some of these:
- Enable "parental controls" on smartphones and other screen devices. Check with the manufacturers or your carrier about blocking inappropriate web content. You can find articles on the web about setting parental controls on the more common phones. Simply Google: "how to set parental controls on [insert phone type]."
- Parents have full access to kids' phones and text messages at any time. Use of phones and other screens are a privilege, not a right.
- No friending people you haven't met face to face.
- Don't post locations ever when home or alone. (Do you really want everyone to know where you live or that you're about to walk to your car alone?) Don't let everyone see where you are at any given moment on Snapmaps.
- Parents can view Netflix "viewing activity" at any time, and it's not spying.
- Phones are turned off at night (best to pick a specific time that works for your family) and plugged into a universal docking station where all the phones go "to rest for the night."

Let's face it; this little device is a Swiss Army Knife of technology... and it goes with them everywhere!

NOTE: The first bullet point in the previous list doesn't have to be on your list of "guardrails." Enabling parental controls is just a good step to take that will help protect your kid. It isn't a rule—it's simply a practice parents should consider prior to buying a phone for their children.

Doug: Jonathan's book, The Teen's Guide to Social Media & Mobile Devices, is excellent for helping your kids understand some of these guardrails. He spends entire chapters on key areas like the photos they're posting, the people they're friending, and the affirmation they're seeking. Great book to read with your kids!

Both of Us: Today's smartphone is unique. It's a phone, a computer, a GPS, a camera, a game system, a calendar, a clock, a flashlight, a music player… and it's the preferred social networking tool. Let's face it: This little device is a Swiss Army Knife of technology—and it goes with your kids… everywhere!

When our kids learned to drive, we literally spent months training them, counseling them, and warning them about the dangers. We drove with them and slowly allowed them to have a chance behind the wheel. We made them study laws, and our government required them to pass certain skills tests to drive legally. Driving is a big deal.

But when our 13-year-old wants a smartphone—a handheld computer more powerful than the ones that guided Apollo 11 to the moon—we often just hand it to him saying, "Enjoy!" (or perhaps more accurately, "Now I don't have to hear you complain anymore!")

Like a car, today's phones almost necessitate their own list of rules and training. Hopefully we won't just hand our kids a phone without any guidance. And much like we wouldn't give our teenager a car without brakes, we probably shouldn't hand our 11-year-old boy or girl one of these phones without some specific parental controls.

Many wise families opt to use a phone contract when their kids first get phones. Phone contracts are very effective when a child doesn't have a phone yet. We find that kids will often "do anything" to get a phone. A parent can use a phone contract as a very effective bargaining tool:

"Well, I don't know if you're ready for a phone yet. The phone requires a lot of responsibility."
"Oh, I'm really responsible!"

"Well, it might tempt you to stay up late texting and distract you from face-to-face relationships. I don't think you should have a phone until you're ready to show responsibility in many areas."

"I would totally do that! Pleeeeeeeeeeeease."

"Well, the only way I would let you get a phone is if you agreed to a phone contract."

"Sure!"

"And… rubbing my feet every night for a year!"

Most studies reveal the majority of today's kids want a phone more than they want a car. This gives parents strong negotiating clout. We encourage you to use that power and have them sign a phone contract. We've provided a sample contract on page 62 (as well as other phone and media information in the Appendices).

Sadly, the majority of parents don't have conversations with their kids about being responsible with their phones. We know of a mother who experienced a living nightmare with her daughter who met a guy using social media on her phone. It started when her daughter "friended" a boy she didn't know through one of her social networks. The two developed a friendship and eventually phone numbers were exchanged. After weeks of texting, this boy began engaging in more intimate conversations—and finally he sent her an inappropriate photo. He pleaded for her to do the same, and she refused. Mom finally stumbled on her daughter's phone, saw the photo, and freaked out. This, of course, led to the question, "Where did you know this kid from?"

"I met him on social media."

Long story short. It wasn't a kid. The police now have her phone, and they're posing as the teenage girl trying to catch this pedophile.

I wish we were making this story up.

Are you one of the "all too many" parents who've never had the conversation with your kids about their online profile? Have you discussed "friending" strangers? Have you talked with them about turning off "location services"? (See Appendix C for more on this.)

If you don't use an actual contract with your kids, at least have multiple conversations with them about being responsible with their phones. Warn them of the dangers. We've included a conversation guide for you, "Talking with Your Teenagers About Social Media & Their Phone" in Appendix C.

If your kids have several years left in your home and have already been give access to phones, yes, this might be a harder sell. But we still recommend some type of use contract or agreement. You'd implement this contract the same way you'd bring up proposed guardrails—cautiously—and with their input throughout the process. And always remember: Use of a phone—and other devices with screens and Internet access—is a privilege, not a right.

As your kids grow older and begin to demonstrate trust in these areas, you can slowly segue toward lighter guidance. Extreme, unrealistic, legalistic, or over-protective guardrails often steer kids toward rebellion.

Are you one of the 54% of parents who have never had the conversation with your kids about their online profile?

Honest Thoughts:
Have you enabled any parental controls on your kids' phones or computers or other devices with screens and Internet access—and talked with them about their online profiles on social networking sites? Why or why not?

_____

_____

_____

_____

Are any of the above sample phone guardrails worth considering in your home? Why or why not?

_____

_____

_____

_____

The bold statement above reads: "Extreme, unrealistic, legalistic, or over-protective guardrails often steer kids toward rebellion." Have you seen examples of this in your home? Give an example.

_____

_____

_____

_____

Where do you think the balance lies in your home between "realistic" and "unrealistic" guardrails? What does this look like?

_____

_____

_____

_____

We've heard it said, "Rules without relationship lead to rebellion." So let's consider this third step in proactive parenting…

3. Talk as You Walk

Some of the best parenting advice we've ever read was written several thousand years ago. Moses instructed his people to love God with all their heart, soul and strength (Deut. 6). But he didn't stop there. Moses also told them to impress these commandments on their children when they sit at home, as they walk along the road, when they lie down and when they get up (v. 7).

That's quite a mandate: Having conversations with your kids about God's love morning, noon and night—while you're sitting, walking, getting ready for bed and getting up in the morning. Moses paints a clear picture of parents who regularly instruct their children as they go through life together.

We don't want to sound like fanatics here, but this is where the media has really lied to our kids. Almost every kids' TV show portrays shrewd, savvy peers who figure out life for themselves with little, if any, help from their oblivious parents. These TV brats leave their parents on the sidelines because, let's face it… "parents are clueless idiots who just don't understand kids today."

This typecasting is the polar opposite of biblical teaching, which — like the entire book of Proverbs—encourages children to humbly learn from their parents and heed their instruction.

But the blame doesn't rest solely upon the Disney Channel. Parents are neglecting their calling to "talk as we walk."

Moses gave us the mandate to talk with our kids morning, noon and night… walking, sitting on the couch, eating dinner… you name it!

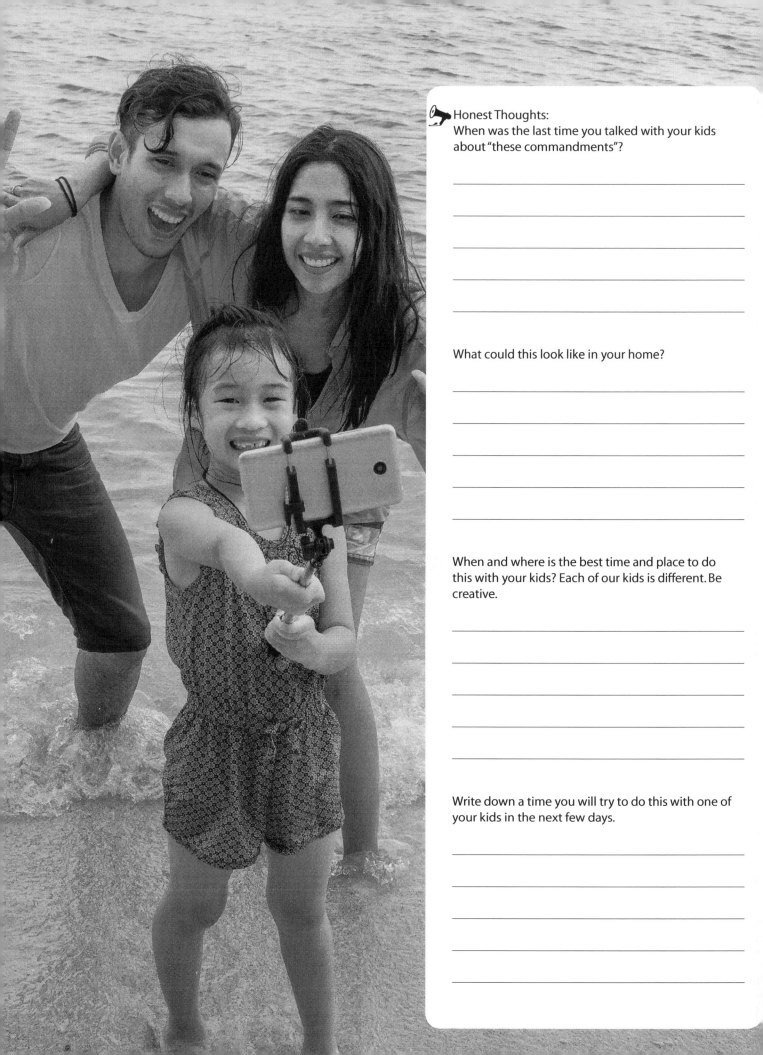

Honest Thoughts:
When was the last time you talked with your kids about "these commandments"?

_____

_____

_____

_____

_____

What could this look like in your home?

_____

_____

_____

_____

_____

When and where is the best time and place to do this with your kids? Each of our kids is different. Be creative.

_____

_____

_____

_____

_____

Write down a time you will try to do this with one of your kids in the next few days.

_____

_____

_____

_____

_____

Proactive parenting efforts like building strong values, setting realistic guardrails and engaging in frequent conversations can save a world of hurt. But do they keep our kids from ever veering off course?

Nope. Sorry! Wish we could guarantee complete obedience.

Sometimes our kids will push the limits with chores, behavior, school, homework, and screens (one of their favorite—and easiest—ways to do this).

So how can parents respond appropriately when our kids violate our trust?

Caring Enough to Carry Out Consequences— Responding When They Mess Up

Earlier in this book we discussed the principle of seguing from heavy guidance to lighter guidance as our kids grow and become more mature, giving them the opportunity to make decisions on their own. Parents feel confortable doing this when their kids demonstrate responsible behavior and earn more of trust. And we reward their good choices with more freedom.

But what about when they aren't making good choices? What about when they break through the guardrails we've carefully set?

When our kids bust through our guardrails, consequences are necessary. Here are some tips for enforcing consequences when our kids push the limits and break the rules.

1. Delay Punishment
This is solid parenting advice. When our kids break a rule, don't punish them that very second. A parent's anger is usually too apparent, and words are spoken that are difficult to erase hours later when cooler heads prevail. Address the issue immediately, but make them wait for the punishment.

This brilliant move achieves two desired results:

    A. It gives parents much-needed time to cool off!

    B. This "delay" is punishment in itself. Instead of just getting it over with, tell them (calmly… remember, yelling doesn't work), "I really don't know exactly what I'm going to do yet. Just leave your phone on my dresser, and we'll talk in a few hours about what's going to happen." Kids hate this, and it forces them to think about their choices and possible consequences while they wait.

But eventually you have to come up with a consequence. So when you do…

2. Make the Consequence Match the Violation
Don't think up random consequences. When at all possible, use natural consequences, or consequences that match the infraction.

If your kids break their phones, have them pay for it. Welcome to the real world, junior! We realize this may appear harsh to some, but consequences are a significant part of learning

to grow up. If it's too costly for them to afford, then have them pay for half of it, and let them know you're willing to own the punishment with them, paying for the other half. But let them experience the pain of real-world consequences. We aren't helping them if we constantly swoop down and save them from real-life problems.

Children who are constantly "saved" are the ones who grow into teens who believe nothing is ever their fault. It's always the stupid teacher, coach, advisor, driver, friend… and yes, parent. Why expect them to take responsibility when they've never had to?

Let's say your daughter downloaded a social media app that you forbid. You could take away her phone for a given time. Or if it's the first time she's done something like this, and you think she learned her lesson, you could say it like this:

"I'm not going to take away your phone this time. This time, you get grace. You're just going to delete that app. But next time you violate this rule, the consequence is going to be more severe [or, better yet, articulate the severe consequence so it's known ahead of time]."

Or let's say your son browses some racy websites. First, talk with him about it, but don't make him feel dirty or perverted. Guilt isn't a long-term motivator. Let him know that these desires are normal and use this as an opportunity to tell him the explicit truth about sex. After the conversation, ask him what he thinks would be a fair consequence to help him learn to respect the guardrails you set… which leads to our next tip…

3. Ask Them to Set Their Own Consequences
When our kids violate a guardrail, ask them what they think an appropriate punishment would be.

We've done this at times because we honestly couldn't think of anything. Funny, our kids usually come up with something really good. Just put on your best poker face and agree, "Excellent thinking. What do you think this consequence will teach you?" This gives our kids a chance to dialogue with us about what they've learned.

Which leads to our next tip…

4. Look for Teachable Moments
Far more important than any punishment is the conversation you have about the punishment. Yes, this is living out Deuteronomy 6, as mentioned earlier: Talk as You Walk.

Let's go back to the phone scenario: Sometimes our kids won't even realize the danger they're flirting with on their phones. Whenever you encounter a story in the news about a kid making poor decisions, bring it up at dinner, and (don't lecture) just ask questions. "Why do you think this girl got into this situation?" "How might she have avoided this in the first place?" (The family dinner is one of those great communication arenas where healthy conversations can flow. Do your best to make those meals a priority.)

Parents can do the same with a pause button on the remote control when they see one of these teachable moments while watching TV or a movie.

There have been times where our kids have messed up pretty bad and brought natural consequences upon themselves. At times like this, we often just say something like: "It seems like you're already facing some pretty nasty, natural consequences. I probably don't need to add any more into the mix, right?" Your kids probably won't disagree with this. So propose, "Just tell me what you've learned from this situation and how you'll choose to prevent it from happening again." After discussing this for a while, you can add, "What can I do to help you from getting into this situation again?"

All of these tips are good, but this final step is essential…

5. Demonstrate Unmistakable Love

The key word here is "unmistakable." Don't assume your children know you love them while you're yelling at them and confiscating their phones! Make it so "unmistakably" obvious that you love them—and that their consequence is only to help them avoid veering off course.

Sometimes we need to really demonstrate a bold selflessness to model this kind of love. It's an interesting balance. It's bold because we aren't going to wimp out and let them do whatever they want. But it's selfless because we're willing to invest time and money to help them succeed.

This might mean giving up on some of our own activities to hang out with them when they're grounded. You can experience some great father-son time when he's restricted from his video games; since there's nothing else he can do, he'll hang out with you.

Parents don't earn popularity points when they punish their kids by following through with consequences, but effective parenting isn't about winning popularity contests. It's about loving them enough to follow through, and caring about them enough to be there to lift them up when they're down.

Parenting is very difficult. Sometimes our kids will continue to push the limits, compelling us to continue enforcing consequences. But don't give up. Consistency is important. And no matter what, don't forget tip #5—demonstrate unmistakable love. If we practice the first four, but have not love, we're just a gong or a clanging cymbal (a loose interpretation of 1 Corinthians 13).

What about you?

Honest Thoughts:
Have you ever used any of these methods before? How did it work?

_____
_____
_____
_____
_____
_____

Which of these tips might be most helpful in your home? Explain.

_____
_____
_____
_____
_____
_____
_____

How do you think your kids will respond if you implement these kinds of consequences to their disobedience?

_____
_____
_____
_____
_____
_____

Summarize this chapter in your own words.

_____
_____
_____
_____
_____
_____

THE JOURNEY AHEAD

Luckily for us, the process doesn't start at "enforcing consequences." The process starts when our kids are young, and we're helping them choose which road to embark on. All these consequences and guardrails are only as good as the road we take.

Navigating these roads as a parent isn't easy, but let's be honest: Navigating these roads as a child is far more difficult! Parents have the awesome privilege to come alongside their children on this journey to adulthood, offering care and counsel. The difficult part is knowing how much of the latter to provide.

We hope the words in this book have been an encouragement to you in this journey as a parent:
   • We've looked at the map and realized we need directions (Chapter 1).
   • We agreed it would be ridiculous to focus on guardrails without first considering where the road was going. So we spent some time thinking about our values and how our rules and standards will flow from those values (Chapter 2).
   • We plotted our course, planning a journey from heavy guidance to lighter guidance (Chapter 3).
   • We set realistic and helpful guardrails (Chapter 4).
   • We introduced those guardrails to our family (Chapter 5).
   • We cared enough to carry out consequences when rules were broken (Chapter 6).

This whole process was bathed in conversation.

So what now?

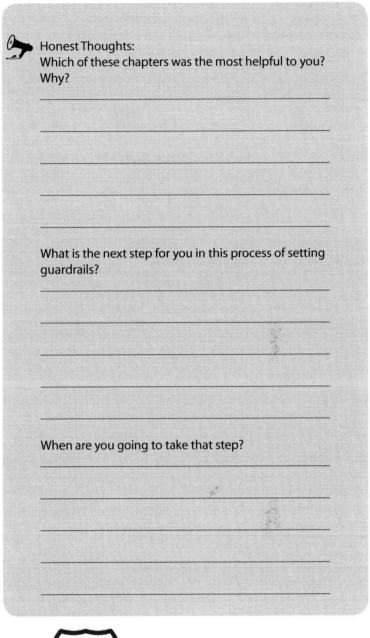

Honest Thoughts:
Which of these chapters was the most helpful to you? Why?

_____
_____
_____
_____
_____

What is the next step for you in this process of setting guardrails?

_____
_____
_____
_____
_____

When are you going to take that step?

_____
_____
_____
_____
_____

SIDE BAR

Sande, mother of two teenagers in a blended family writes: It's amazing how some of the best bonding time we've had with our kids was when they were grounded.

My stepson is "grounded" from the xbox right now. He wasn't happy about this, of course, but within a few days we started noticing him hanging around with us because he's bored.

I came home last night to find he and his dad chasing each other around the house with those plastic guns that shoot little plastic darts.

It was fun to see them laughing and having fun. (I might just have to ground him a little longer!)

You can make an amazing impact in the life of your kids, loving them, coaching them, and helping them learn to navigate this road to adulthood. The journey won't be without mishaps. Kids will bust through guardrails, and you'll have to respond in love, consequences… and plenty of conversation. But hopefully these principles will help you along that journey… they might even save you from smashing your kid's phone!

APPENDIX C
SMALL GROUP DISCUSSION QUESTIONS FOR EACH CHAPTER

These questions are designed to trigger helpful dialogue and discussion about the content of each chapter. Feel free to use one, or all, or none, or write your own questions. The goal isn't to have one right answer, the goal is to engage with others who are facing similar issues where you can learn and help one another.

CHAPTER 1:

1. The authors mentioned the good ol' days of CB radios, black & white TVs, and curfews. What were some of the rules or guardrails you had as a kid?

2. Which boundaries did you rebel against the most when you were young?

3. How did your parents respond? How did that work out?

4. What are some struggles—that you mentioned in your reflection writing for this chapter—you're having right now regarding setting up or enforcing guardrails in your home?

5. How have you been responding to this situation? How's that working for you?

6. Explain the distinction the authors made between rules and guardrails.

7. What's one example of a guardrail you've already set up that might be working to keep your kids on course?

CHAPTER 2:

1. What are some values you would like to pass on to your kids?

2. How do you feel about the authors' idea that values are more important than rules? Agree/Disagree? Why?

3. Give an example why arbitrary rules fall short.

4. The authors listed several instances when values can be taught, such teaching God's word in the home, taking kids to church, discipling them, and allowing them to be mentored by other positive adult role models. What are some examples of what any of these practices might look like in your home?

5. Could your kids use a heavier dose of any of the above (see question 4) practices? Which areas?

6. How should parents respond if their kids resist these types of influences?

7. What's one way you can try to teach your kids values this week?

CHAPTER 3:

1. What are some of the landmarks you've already observed in your parenting journey?

2. What do you like and/or dislike about Jonathan's No Rules by Age 17½?

3. Which of the two parenting extremes (overprotective or overly permissive) best represents the way you were raised? Offer an example.

4. Which of these two extremes do you probably lean toward now that you're a parent (because let's be honest: no one is in the dead center)? Why do you think you lean this way?

5. Give an example of what "incremental independence" probably should look like in your parenting.

6. What does incremental independence actually look like in your home?

7. What's one area that you soon could "release the grip" a little with your kids, helping them learn to make decisions for themselves? What will that look like? How difficult will that be?

CHAPTER 4:

1. Which of the pre-guardrail considerations stirred your thinking the most? Why?

2. The authors recommended "co-viewing" entertainment media as a guardrail ("Let's look up this movie and see what it's about. Then let's watch it together and discuss it.") How can parents use a tool like co-viewing to stimulate dialogue as opposed to a long, parental monologue?

3. Which of the authors' personal guardrails did you like? Why?

4. Which of the authors' personal guardrails are probably not a fit for your family? Why?

5. What's one other guardrail you listed—in your reflection writing from this chapter— that you might want to adopt? How do you see this working with your family?

6. What's one guardrail that you've heard from someone in your group today that you really like and may want to add to your list?

CHAPTER 5:

1. Describe how "family meetings" might look in your home?

2. The authors recommended slowly walking into the "rules pool" rather than setting off an out-of-nowhere cannonball to introduce your guardrails. What do you think this will actually look like in your family?

3. What are some specific ways we can remember to involve our entire family in this process of setting guardrails so they're prepared when we finally propose them?

4. Where is a fun environment you might choose to have this family meeting?

5. What attitudes or negative responses might you encounter? How do you envision responding to these?

6. What's something you can do to prepare for the feedback you might receive?

CHAPTER 6:

1. How can teaching our kids good values help them make better decisions with their technology? Give a specific example.

2. What are some specific guardrails you hope will help keep your kids on course?

3. Researchers found only about half of parents use any parental controls on their kids' computers, and less than half talked with their kids at all about their online profile on social networking sites. Why do you think so many parents haven't set these guardrails or had these discussions?

4. Read the resources in the Appendices that help you set phone guardrails and have discussions about phone safety. What are some issues these resources bring to light that you need to discuss in your home?

5. Are there any guardrails you have right now that might be too strict? If so, what changes might you make?

6. Share with the group in what ways you've had difficulty enforcing consequences. Why can this be difficult for you?

7. Which of the authors' tips for enforcing consequences was the most helpful to you? Explain.

This discussion guide was written specifically for this book by Adam McLane, author of "A Parent's Guide to Understanding Social Media."

The following is a discussion guide parents can use to talk with their teenagers about being responsible with the extremely powerful little device they carry around in their pockets… their phones. Rather than focus on what our teenagers can and cannot do, let's instead focus on what's a good idea and what's not a good idea. Share these ideas with your teenagers and discuss each one:

1. It's a good idea to "friend" people you've met and not "friend" people you haven't met. About two-thirds of teenagers have phones that connects to the Internet. With that, you'll have access to a bunch of ways to connect with people on social networks. Since people often pose as people they aren't, it's probably a good idea to connect online only with people you've actually met in person

2. It isn't a good idea to use location services. Most new phones have applications that will add your location when you post a status or a photo. By default, it's better if you don't turn on that feature. You don't want to post photos that show strangers where you are, who you're with, or what stuff you have. That can lead to personal safety problems or even make you a target for theft.

3. It's a good idea to text your parents when you're somewhere you normally aren't. You probably have a regular routine. But sometimes things change, right? Let's say you normally have soccer practice after school, but it got cancelled so you went over to a friend's house. It's a great use of your phone to tell your parents about that change in plans.

4. It isn't a good idea to sleep with your phone. A major problem for schools is students not getting enough sleep. Your body needs more sleep than the average adult, but most teenagers actually get less sleep than their parents! Do yourself a favor and turn your phone off at night, charge it somewhere so it's far enough away from you that it won't bother you until you're ready for breakfast. Trust me, those texts or notifications from friends can wait.

5. It's a good idea to use your phone in the living room instead of your bedroom. In almost every instance, when people are using their phones to look at things they aren't supposed to or doing things that aren't good for them, they're in private places inside their home. Make it a habit to use your phone in common areas of your home.

6. It isn't a good idea to break your phone just to get a new one. Sounds silly, right? But we know sometimes a phone gets "accidentally" dropped so that the screen cracks or "somehow" falls in the toilet when a new phone (one you'd rather have) is now on the market. Sure, accidents happen. But if you want to get a different phone, just have a rational conversation with your parents instead of destroying the one you already have.

7. It's a good idea to always assume that everything on your phone could become public. It's easy to assume that because "its yours" or because it has a password that whatever happens on your phone is private. It isn't. In fact, everything you do online or with your phone is traceable back to you. Every text you send, every photo you send or receive, everything you like, repost, message, or even read is recorded… forever. In fact, not only is what you send and who you send it to traceable, so is your exact location when you send it. So be wise. One day it could all be public. You can delete it from your phone or even get a new phone. But it's still there.

APPENDIX C
**THE FOLLOWING IS A SAMPLE CONTRACT BETWEEN PARENTS AND KIDS THAT CAN EASILY BE ADAPTED FOR YOUR FAMILY.
THIS CONTRACT IS DOWNLOADABLE AT:
PARENTSSMASHINGPHONES.COM**

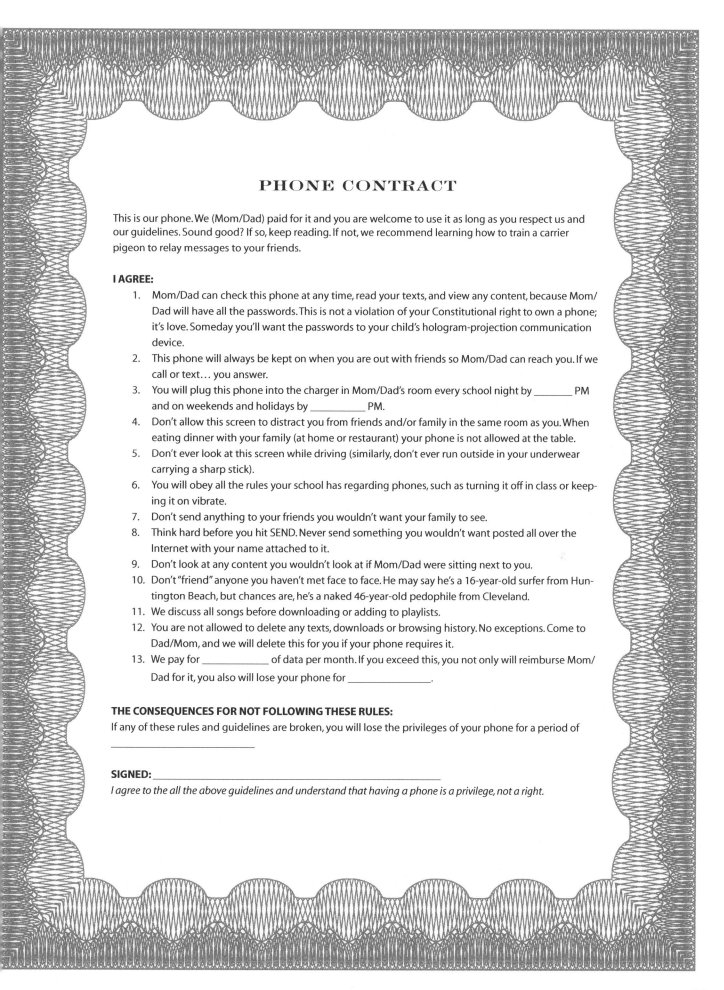

PHONE CONTRACT

This is our phone. We (Mom/Dad) paid for it and you are welcome to use it as long as you respect us and our guidelines. Sound good? If so, keep reading. If not, we recommend learning how to train a carrier pigeon to relay messages to your friends.

I AGREE:

1. Mom/Dad can check this phone at any time, read your texts, and view any content, because Mom/Dad will have all the passwords. This is not a violation of your Constitutional right to own a phone; it's love. Someday you'll want the passwords to your child's hologram-projection communication device.
2. This phone will always be kept on when you are out with friends so Mom/Dad can reach you. If we call or text… you answer.
3. You will plug this phone into the charger in Mom/Dad's room every school night by _____ PM and on weekends and holidays by _____ PM.
4. Don't allow this screen to distract you from friends and/or family in the same room as you. When eating dinner with your family (at home or restaurant) your phone is not allowed at the table.
5. Don't ever look at this screen while driving (similarly, don't ever run outside in your underwear carrying a sharp stick).
6. You will obey all the rules your school has regarding phones, such as turning it off in class or keeping it on vibrate.
7. Don't send anything to your friends you wouldn't want your family to see.
8. Think hard before you hit SEND. Never send something you wouldn't want posted all over the Internet with your name attached to it.
9. Don't look at any content you wouldn't look at if Mom/Dad were sitting next to you.
10. Don't "friend" anyone you haven't met face to face. He may say he's a 16-year-old surfer from Huntington Beach, but chances are, he's a naked 46-year-old pedophile from Cleveland.
11. We discuss all songs before downloading or adding to playlists.
12. You are not allowed to delete any texts, downloads or browsing history. No exceptions. Come to Dad/Mom, and we will delete this for you if your phone requires it.
13. We pay for _____ of data per month. If you exceed this, you not only will reimburse Mom/Dad for it, you also will lose your phone for _____.

THE CONSEQUENCES FOR NOT FOLLOWING THESE RULES:

If any of these rules and guidelines are broken, you will lose the privileges of your phone for a period of

_____

SIGNED: _____

I agree to the all the above guidelines and understand that having a phone is a privilege, not a right.

WRITE YOUR OWN PHONE CONTRACT IDEAS HERE

The blogosphere is currently bursting at the seams with insightful posts and articles from parenting authors providing helpful social media rules and guidelines for their teens and tweens—everything from iPhone rules and Instagram guidelines to general social media parenting advice on how to monitor your teenagers' online activity (in a world where Facebook is just one of many choices).

I've been using some of these articles as discussion springboards with my daughters. After all, the one common denominator almost all this research shares is the advice to parents to regularly dialogue about this issue with their kids.

Ashley—my youngest—was of course all "sighs" during these conversations. If I brought up social media, she rolled her eyes, exhaled loudly, and proclaimed, "Dad, have you ever had any problem with me and this stuff? No. Then relax!"

If I only had a dime for every time my daughter told me to relax.

Yesterday, after asking Ashley a little about Instagram and showing her an article with parental guidelines, she sighed, rolled her eyes, and informed me that it's parents who really need a list of rules for social media: "Because if parents expect us to talk with them about this stuff, they need to not be so dorky."

"Oh really?" I asked, trying not to sound defensive.

"Relax, Dad. I'm not talking about you. It's those creepy parents!"

Then she began to list her rules.

NOTE: When she said them, she was just ranting to me, but I started quickly taking notes (which was pretty difficult while rolling on the floor laughing). She didn't intend for me to post this rant. It was only afterward when I asked, "Can I post these?" that she agreed—for a small price.

So pardon her sarcastic tone. Just think of this as the things-teenagers-might-want-to-tell-us-but-never-do.

So here they are, and I guess when you read them… you'll know if you're a creepy parent or not… according to Ashley.

ASHLEY'S SOCIAL MEDIA RULES FOR CREEPY PARENTS

1. Don't sit on Facebook all day. It's easy to see who is and isn't on Facebook all day. Some parents are obviously on it waaaaaaaay more than kids. Don't you have a life?

2. Don't comment on everything we post. If you were there or have something unique to offer, then fine. But please don't comment on every picture posted by every teenager you know. It's a little creepy.

3. Don't try to talk like you're 16. You aren't. Act your age. Embrace the fact that you're 45. Talk 45. Be 45. We like you as 45.

4. If sexting is a problem, I haven't seen it. Please don't tell me that Snapchat is only for sexting. I use Snapchat all the time with my friends showing them my facial expressions for fun. I've never sent or received a sexy pic in my life. Chill!

5. Don't LIKE every picture we post. See Rule #2.

6. And definitely don't comment on your kids' friends' pictures or posts. That's sort of six-degrees-of-separation creepy.

7. Stop stalking your kids on Facebook. "Who was that kid you were sitting next to at the football game in the orange shirt?" Creepy! How would you like it if I asked you, "Who was that lady in the low-cut top you were talking with by the copy machine at work today?" It's okay to keep up with us on Facebook… but stop spying on us.

I was guilty of one of these. One out of seven isn't bad, right? Does that make me creepy?

Alyssa—the oldest of my two daughters—agreed with most of these, but inserted, "Yeah, but just because Ashley has never used Snapchat for bad doesn't mean that all kids are innocent of that. Parents need to know their kids." She also added, "It's okay when some of my friends' parents comment on my pictures or posts. That's nice. Just not every picture and post."

NOTES:

TWO PARENTING WORKSHOPS

Bring Doug, Jonathan… or both… to your church, your organization or your community!
Parenting in a Screen-Saturated Culture Workshop
More Information, Dates & Registration at: DougFields.com

OTHER BOOKS BY THESE AUTHORS:

Available at DougFields.com:

Fresh Start:
God's Invitation to a Great Life

Refuel:
An Uncomplicated Guide to Connecting with God

- -

Available at JonathanMcKeeWrites.com:

Candid Confessions of an Imperfect Parent:
Building Relationships, Buying Breakfasts, and
Other Secrets for Connecting with Your Teenager

Connect:
Real Relationships in a World of Isolation

Made in the USA
San Bernardino, CA
12 July 2019